BASKETBALL'S
HALL OF FAME

BASKETBALL'S HALL OF FAME

BY SANDY PADWE

An Associated Features Book

tempo books

GROSSET & DUNLAP, INC.
A National General Company
Publishers   New York

Published Simultaneously in Canada

ISBN: 0-448-05575-9

Tempo Books is Registered in the U. S. Patent Office

Tempo Books Edition

Printed in the United States of America

For Coach John Egli of Penn State, whose patience and friendship with an inexperienced student reporter always will be remembered.

Acknowledgments

The author wishes to express his thanks to all those who have assisted in the preparation of this book, especially Zander Hollander of Associated Features Inc. and Lee Williams, Executive Director of the Basketball Hall of Fame. The author also wishes to express his thanks to the Philadelphia *Inquirer* for use of its library.

The following source materials were used in preparation of this book and the author expresses his appreciation; *the Cavalcade of Basketball* by Alexander M. Weyand; *24 Seconds to Shoot* by Leonard Koppett; *Basketball's Greatest Teams* by Al Hirshberg; *Red Auerbach, Winning the Hard Way* by Paul Sann; *50 Years of Basketball* by Joe Lapchick; *Better Basketball* by Forrest C. Allen; *Basketball, Its Origin and Development* by Dr. James Naismith.

Also, *Sport* magazine, *Sports Illustrated, The Sporting News, The Saturday Evening Post, Colliers, The New York Times,* Phillips Petroleum Co.; University of Illinois; Oklahoma State University; University of Indiana; Stanford University; St. Louis University, and the National Basketball Association.

Sandy Padwe

CONTENTS

Foreword

When the Basketball Hall of Fame first opened its doors to the public early in 1968, another milestone in the world of sport had been reached. Basketball, the only international sport truly an American creation, finally had a home for its heroes.

It wasn't long before it became apparent that an official book was needed to document the entire Hall of Fame story and the contributions of its members.

Work was begun toward this end and now the book, *Basketball's Hall of Fame,* has become a reality. The writer, Sandy Padwe, is a talented sports columnist for the Philadelphia *Inquirer* and has long been identified with the basketball scene. He tells the story with warmth and color as well as with adherence to fact.

I am delighted that the public now has this official book documenting the Basketball Hall of Fame.

Lee Williams
Executive Director and Curator
Basketball Hall of Fame

Introduction

In 1936, the father of basketball, Dr. James Naismith, took a trip sponsored by the National Association of Basketball Coaches to the Olympic Games in Berlin. When he arrived home, Dr. Naismith, a frugal man, returned the money that remained from his expenses. "Here," he said, "why don't you start a Hall of Fame?"

Dr. Naismith was an extremely modest man who never dreamed that some day there really would be a Hall of Fame, and that it would be named for him. When he made his suggestion, he was simply planting an idea.

"He never realized the impact of the game," said Lee Williams, executive director of the Hall of Fame. "In 1937, he went to a doubleheader at Madison Square Garden and he saw 18,000 pay their way in. His reaction was, 'Good heavens, all these people would come to watch a basketball game?'

"To him, basketball was a means to an end: physical training, the use of leisure time. He was a typical teacher and he remained that way until he died."

The coaches' association thought Naismith's idea was excellent and it gave the proper backing from the very beginning. Upon his death in 1939, the NABC issued a formal proposal calling for the construction of a Hall of Fame on the campus of Springfield College,

Springfield, Mass., where Dr. Naismith invented the game.

Due to World War II, the project had a difficult, sporadic beginning, and it wasn't until 1948 that Edward J. Hickox, former Springfield College coach and a friend of Dr. Naismith in Springfield, became the unpaid executive director of the Hall of Fame project.

Springfield College gave Hickox an office in the Student Counseling Center and he hired Mrs. Ruth Silvia as his secretary. Hickox and Mrs. Silvia were the permanent staff until 1963 when Hickox was succeeded by Clifford Wells, who served until June 1966. During this period the NABC underwrote the entire budget for the Hall of Fame, over $100,000.

Fund-raising was slow and difficult. Then in 1966, Williams, a former president of the coaches' association, became executive director of the Hall of Fame. When Williams arrived, only the foundation of the building existed. A year later, Williams had raised enough money so that construction could begin on the handsome, rectangular, red-brick building at the east end of the Springfield campus.

Williams, a pleasant, enthusiastic individual, coached Colby College to a 252–190 record from 1946 through 1966. "The Hall of Fame Trustees," he said, "came to me early in June 1966 and asked if I would be interested in becoming executive director of the Hall of Fame. I agreed and arrived in Springfield in September. I felt that the Basketball Hall of Fame was as important to the athletic world as a new church to its flock."

Williams concentrated his fund-raising drive in the national basketball community in general and around Springfield in particular.

On February 17, 1968, the Naismith Memorial Basketball Hall of Fame opened for a preview and the following day the public was admitted for the first time. It had taken a great deal of time, effort and money, but Dr. Naismith's idea was now reality.

The Mosler lobby is the first inside view of the Hall of Fame. Edward Mosler, a member of the Board of Trustees, also donated many of the basketball uniforms that are in the Hall of Fame.

There is a special section dedicated to Dr. Naismith in the lobby, dominated by an enlarged photogaraph of the game's founder. Adjoining the lobby is the reception area, known as the Hall of Founders. On the Founders' Wall are 1,600 names of coaches, officials, individuals, small groups and large companies, all of whom donated a minimum of $100 to the building fund. More than one hundred colleges, which donated $1,000 each, are also listed.

Dr. Naismith was a deeply religious man and the Hall of Fame's Board of Trustees and the executive director remembered this when they designed the Honors Court, home of each Hall of Fame member.

The Honors Court was meant to look as much like a cathedral as possible, and the designers succeeded. Each member of the Hall of Fame has his 14-inch portrait superimposed in the middle of a multicolored hand-painted, 10-foot-high piece of lucite plastic. The effect is that of a stained-glass window, with light coming from behind colorfully illuminating the plaque.

There is a brief biography beneath each photograph of the Hall of Fame members. The displays are in order of election.

In addition to the individuals, four teams are in the Hall of Fame, and these teams are honored with photographs. They are the first team to play the game at Springfield College, the Original Celtics, the Buffalo YMCA Germans and the Original Renaissance of New York.

From the Honors Court one passes directly into the Museum, where there is a replica of the gymnasium where the first game was played in 1891. The replica is complete with the running track that encircled basketball courts in the early years.

Dr. Naismith's original 13 rules are on display below the peach basket first used and nailed to the bottom of the track, 10 feet high.

The purpose of the museum is to trace chronologically the history of the game, from the first set of rules and the first basket to the modern day. Included in the museum are displays of the uniforms, equipment and pictures. These displays—uniforms worn by such basketball stars as Wilt Chamberlain, Bill Russell, Bob Davies, Ernie Calverley, Joe Fulks, George Mikan, Ed Macauley, Cazzi Russell, Bill Bradley, Bob Cousy and Elvin Hayes—are openly displayed. "We wanted the people to be able to get a flavor of the game's history from these uniforms," Williams said. "And we didn't want them locked up. We wanted them out where they could be closer to the people."

The uniforms give a sense of history because most of them were worn during some of the game's greatest moments. Chamberlain's uniform is the one he wore on the night he scored 100 points; Calverley's uniform is the one he wore on the night that he made his 58-foot shot in the National Invitation Tournament against Bowling Green; Macauley's is the one he wore the night he scored his 10,000th professional point, and so on.

Interspersed among the uniform displays are pieces of basketball memorabilia such as the ball used by Jerry Harkness when he made a 92-foot basket in an American Basketball Association game. The largest pair of basketball shoes also are on display. They belong to Bob Lanier, the All-American center from St. Bonaventure: size 20. The ball that Wilt Chamberlain used when he scored his 25,000th point is at the Hall of Fame, as is the ball he used when he set the record for 37 consecutive field goals (during a four-game span).

There is a section devoted entirely to international basketball that includes autographed balls by the various winning U.S. Olympic and Pan American teams, including the 1968 Olympic champions in Mexico City.

One of the most unusual displays in the Hall of Fame consists of a surprising number of basketball stamps issued by the countries of the world.

Every bit of basketball history and lore is in the Hall of Fame: from the trophy given to Windsor, Colorado, for winning the National Interscholastic High School Championship in 1924 to the whistle used by official Clarence Jones in the longest game (six overtimes between Niagara and Siena) to Ed Diddle's red crying towel, which became synonymous with basketball at Western Kentucky University.

The Hall of Fame's second floor contains displays on the coaches, officials, writers, and professional and collegiate basketball. There also is a special picture collection of the game's greatest teams, and a colorful set of cartoons depicting memorable moments in the game's history.

The Hickox library also is located on the second floor, where a full-time librarian supervises students who wish to conduct research on the game. Eventually, the library will house the largest collection of basketball history in the world.

A movie and meeting room is located on the lower level of the Hall of Fame. Movies can be selected from the Hall of Fame film library and highlight films are shown at no charge several times daily. A refreshment area also is located adjacent to the theater. The lower level also has displays on the amateurs and high schools.

Williams is director of the museum as well as curator. "How do we collect all these items?" he asked. "We ask for them. Normally we get fine cooperation."

The Honors Committee, consisting of thirteen persons from the various segments of basketball, vote each year on the individuals nominated for the Hall of Fame. John Bunn, the former Stanford and Springfield coach, and a Hall of Famer himself, chairs the Honors Committee. Official nomination forms are available at the Hall of Fame office.

Ten votes of thirteen are needed for election to the Hall of Fame in one of four categories: coach, player, referee and contributor. A coach must have served twenty-five years in the profession to be eligible for election; a player must be retired from active ball for at least five years; and a contributor, an all-inclusive category, can be elected at any time.

"A coach, for example," Williams said, "can be elected to the Hall of Fame under the contributor category. This category was established for people who have made an outstanding contribution to the game in several ways."

The Basketball Hall of Fame differs from baseball's and football's shrines in that it includes all levels of the game; professional, intercollegiate, amateur, military and high school.

The first elections for the Hall of Fame were held in 1959 and at that time the following individuals and teams were honored: Dr. Forrest C. Allen; Dr. Clifford Carlson; Dr. Luther Gulick; Edward J. Hickox; Charles D. Hyatt; Matthew P. Kennedy; Angelo Luisetti; Dr. Walter E. Meanwell; George L. Mikan; Ralph Morgan; Dr. James Naismith; Harold G. Olsen;

John J. Schommer; Amos Alonzo Stagg; Oswald Tower; and the First Team and the Original Celtics.

"You'd be amazed at how many people express surprise that Amos Alonzo Stagg is in the Basketball Hall of Fame," Williams said. "People normally associate him with football without realizing the great part he played in the growth of basketball."

That is just one of the hundreds of surprises the building holds.

1

DR. JAMES NAISMITH
The Inventor

The name of the game easily could have been boxball because James Naismith's original concept called for two boxes to be placed at opposite ends of the first basketball court in the Springfield Armory YMCA, Springfield, Massachusetts.

Shortly before Naismith and eighteen students from the International YMCA Training School were to test the game for the first time, the inventor of basketball still was looking for the proper goals. Naismith spotted the superintendent of the building and asked if he had two boxes about 18 inches square. The superintendent, a man named Stebbins, replied, "No, I haven't any boxes but I'll tell you what I do have. I have two old peach baskets down in the store room if they will do you any good."

"I told him," Naismith said, "to bring them up, and a few minutes later he appeared with two baskets tucked under his arm. They were round and somewhat larger at the top than at the bottom. I found a hammer and some nails and tacked the baskets to the lower rail of the balcony, one at either end of the gym."

That is how basketball started in mid-December 1891 in Springfield, Massachusetts. James Naismith, the inventor, was a young student from the farming country of Almonte, Ontario, Canada. He had been orphaned at the age of eight and a bachelor uncle raised him. Naismith was born November 6, 1861. He was graduated from McGill College, Montreal, in 1887 and then studied at the Presbyterian Theological Seminary for three years. Originally, he wanted to enter the priesthood and actually became an ordained minister in 1915.

Young Naismith, however, had an athletic background. At McGill, he joined the football team. During his senior year there he realized he could combine his love for athletics with his passion for helping mankind.

The vehicle would be the International YMCA Training School, which now is Springfield College. Naismith made his decision not to enter the ministry after talking to Mr. D. A. Budge, secretary of the YMCA in Montreal. "In our conversation," Naismith said, "I brought up the point that I thought that there might be other effective ways of doing good besides preaching. After a while, Budge told me that there was a school in Springfield that was developing men for this field."

At Springfield, Naismith met Dr. Luther Gulick, the man who had a lasting effect on his life. Dr. Gulick was the dean of the physical education school. "He was one of the few men whose teachings have remained with me and have been a help not only in my profession but in my life as well," Naismith said.

Naismith was a student and later a professor at Springfield. One of his colleagues at the school was Amos Alonzo Stagg, who had been a theological student at Yale and who had matriculated at Springfield because he had the same ideas about life as Naismith.

Dr. Gulick introduced the two men. "Stagg," said Naismith forty years later, "grasped my hand with a grip that he was accustomed to use on a baseball, and I retaliated with a grasp that I had learned in wrestling. Our friendship has been a lasting one."

Stagg coached the football team at Springfield, and Naismith, having played rugby and football in Canada, was a natural for the team. He played center, which puzzled him, and one day he asked Stagg why he had placed him at this position. "Jim," Stagg replied, "I play you at center because you can do the meanest things in the most gentlemanly manner."

It was during the summer of 1891 that the students and faculty at Springfield began to realize there was a definite need for new athletic games. "From many different states," Naismith said, "the young men had gathered for the summer term. No matter where they came from, these directors complained that the members of the gymnasium classes were losing interest." Gymnasium classes then consisted mainly of a system of exercise designed to build the body.

"What this new generation wanted," Naismith said, "was pleasure and thrill, as in football, rather than physical benefits only. The students freely discussed these conditions. No one, however, seemed to be able to offer a solution. Dr. Gulick was working desperately on the problem that seemed to threaten the whole subject of physical training, especially in the YMCA."

Naismith also was very concerned. And when, some months later, he was placed in charge of a class whose interest in the gymnasium program was at a low point, he knew he would have to do something to rekindle its imagination.

Two weeks of class-time passed and Naismith was growing desperate. Dr. Gulick was watching him closely. "How I hated the thought of going back and admitting that, after all my theories, I too had failed to hold the interest of the class. All the stubbornness of my Scottish ancestry was aroused, all my pride of achievement urged me on; I would not go back and admit that I had failed," Naismith said.

Naismith returned to his desk and began thinking. He examined the athletic contests of the day such as football, lacrosse, rugby and baseball from every possible angle. "My first generalization," he said, "was that all team games used a ball of some kind; therefore any new game must have a ball. Two kinds of balls were used at that time, one large and the other small. I noted that all games that used a small ball had some intermediate equipment with which to handle it.

"Cricket and baseball had bats, lacrosse and hockey had sticks, tennis and squash had rackets. In each of these games, the use of intermediate equipment made the game more difficult to learn. The Americans were at sea with a lacrosse stick and the Canadians could not use a baseball bat.

"I decided the ball should be large and light, one that could be easily handled and yet could not be concealed. There were two balls of this kind then in use, one the spheroid of rugby and the other the round ball of soccer."

The choice was the rugby ball. But that was only the beginning of Naismith's search for the new game. He then added the theory that since the game was to be played indoors there could be no tackling and there would be no need for the athletes to run with the ball as in rugby or football.

"So far I had a game that was played with a large, light ball; the players could not run with the ball, but must pass it or bat it with the hands; and the pass could be made in any direction," he said.

Naismith then recalled an incident in soccer in which

one player attempted to head the ball just as the other player kicked at it. The result: a badly gashed head. "I could imagine one player attempting to strike the ball with his fist and, intentionally or otherwise, coming in contact with another player's face. I then decided the fist must not be used in striking the ball," Naismith said.

"The next step was to devise some objective for the players. In all existing games there was some kind of goal, and I felt this was essential.

"I thought of the different games . . . football had a goal line and goalposts . . . soccer, lacrosse and hockey had goals into which the ball might be driven. Tennis and badminton had marks on the court inside which the ball must be kept. Thinking of all these, I mentally placed goals at the end of the floor."

His decision on the type of goal followed. As always, his thinking was cool and logical. "If the goal were horizontal instead of vertical," he said, "the players would be compelled to throw the ball in an arc; and force, which made for roughness, would be of no value. I would place a box at either end of the floor, and each time the ball entered the box it would count as a goal.

"There was one thing, however, that I had over-looked. If nine men [his class consisted of eighteen students] formed a defense around the goal, it would be impossible for the ball to enter it; but if I placed the goal above the player's heads, this type of defense would be useless."

Naismith had his game, his equipment and his objective. All he needed was a start for the game, and he came up with the idea of the center jump, again returning to rugby for his idea. It came from that sport's out-of-bounds play where the official took the ball and threw it between two lines of forward players. But Naismith wanted to eliminate the roughness of rugby.

"I reasoned," he said, "that if I picked only one player from each team and threw the ball up between them, there would be little chance for roughness." Thus the center jump.

Among the rules Naismith posted before the first game were the following:

"The goals are a couple of baskets or boxes about 15 inches in diameter across the opening and about 15 inches deep. These are suspended, one at each end of the grounds, about 10 feet from the floor. The object of the game is to put the ball into your opponents' goal. This may be done by throwing the ball from any part of the grounds, with one or both hands, under the following conditions and rules:

"The ball to be an ordinary Association ball.

"1. The ball may be thrown in any direction with one or both hands.

"2. The ball may be batted in any direction with one or both hands (never with the fist).

"3. A player cannot run with the ball. The player must throw it from the spot on which he catches it, allowance to be made for a man who catches the ball when running at a good speed if he tries to stop.

"4. The ball must be held in or between the hands. The arms or body must not be used for holding it.

"5. No shouldering, holding, pushing, tripping or striking in any way the person of an opponent shall be allowed; the first infringement of this rule by any player should count as a foul; the second shall disqualify him until the next goal is made, or, if there was evidence to injure the person, for the whole of the game, no substitute allowed.

"6. A foul is striking at the ball with the fist, violation of Rule 4, 5, and such as described in Rule 6.

"7. If either side makes three consecutive fouls, it shall count a goal for the opponents ('consecutive' means without the opponents in the meantime making a foul).

"8. A goal shall be made when the ball is thrown or batted from the grounds into the basket and stays there, providing those defending the goal do not touch or disturb the goal. If the ball rests on the edge and the opponent moves the basket, it shall count as a goal.

"9. When the ball goes out of bounds, it shall be thrown onto the field of play by the person first touching it. In case of a dispute, the umpire shall throw it straight onto the field. The thrower-in is allowed 5 seconds; if he holds it any longer, it shall go to the opponent. If any side persists in delaying the game, the umpire shall call a foul on that side.

"10. The umpire shall be judge of the men and shall note the fouls and notify the referee when three consecutive fouls have been made. He shall have the power to disqualify men according to Rule 6.

"11. The referee shall be judge of the ball and shall decide when the ball is in play, in bounds, to which side it belongs, and shall keep time. He shall decide when a goal has been made, and keep account of the goals with any other duties that are usually performed by a referee.

"12. The time shall be two 15-minute halves, with 5 minutes' rest between.

"13. The side making the most goals in that time shall be declared the winner. In the case of a draw, the game may, by agreement of the captains, be continued until another goal is made.

"The number composing a team depends largely on the size of the floor space, but it may range from three on a side to forty. The fewer players down to three, the more scientific it may be made, but the more players, the more fun. The men may be arranged according to the idea of the captain, but it has been found that a goalkeeper, two guards, three center men, two wings, and a homeman stationed in the above order from the goal is the best.

"It shall be the duty of the goalkeeper and the two guards to prevent the opponents from scoring. The duty of the wing man and the home man is to put the ball into the opponent's goal, and the center man shall feed the ball forward to the man who has the best opportunity, thus nine men make the best number for a team."

The game proved to be an instant success with the class and news spread quickly of Naismith's new sport. Soon college and townspeople began to watch during their lunch hour and they seemed intrigued. Basketball had its start.

During the Christmas vacation that year, the students returned home and some of them helped start the game at their local YMCAs.

Originally, the students wanted to call the new game Naismith ball. "I laughed," Naismith said, "and told them that I thought that name would kill any game." A student named Frank Mahan from North Carolina then suggested the name "basketball," and Naismith agreed.

Some ten months later, Dr. Gulick, writing in a school periodical, said:

It is doubtful whether a gymnastic game has ever spread so rapidly over the continent as has basketball. It is played from New York to San Francisco and from Maine to Texas by hundreds of teams in associations, athletic clubs and schools. The game is very young and the year's experience has developed certain points which must be more definitely defined. Mr. Naismith is now at work on a new edition of rules.

A year later, the game had spread to a dozen foreign countries. The missionaries were all students of the Springfield school.

As the years passed there were many rule changes. Some of these changes were:

1893—Length of time raised from 15 to 20 minutes per half. Vertical backstop 6x4 required.

1894—Specially manufactured basketballs were introduced.

1895—Baskets enlarged at the top from 15 to 18 inches. Both officials allowed to call fouls. Timers and scorers authorized.

1896—First cage constructed to eliminate problem of ball continually going out of bounds.

Naismith did not remain at Springfield. In 1895 he left for Denver, where he was a director and instructor at the YMCA. He also found time to study for his medical degree, receiving it in 1898 from Gross Medical School. His wife, the former Maude Sherman, also was interested in the game and was one of the first female players.

Later in 1898, Naismith moved to the University of Kansas, where he accepted a position as director of chapel. Then he became a professor of physical education, directing the department until 1925. He continued to teach physical education classes until 1937.

He coached the Kansas basketball team from 1898 to 1907 and his "fun only" approach resulted in a 53–55 record. One of Naismith's pupils, Phog Allen, succeeded him as coach.

He attended nearly every Kansas home game, but was always inconspicuous. A visitor sitting next to the man with the black moustache would never have known that Naismith was the father of the game being played on the floor. Naismith was an observant fan, but a quiet one. He never yelled during a game.

Naismith's life was dedicated to sport, not just basketball. He regarded his "invention" as a mere step in a career devoted to helping mankind enjoy leisure time. He actually believed wrestling was better physical exercise than basketball, and would rather have been off in a corner teaching a student fencing than coaching basketball. A clever tumbler gave him as much pleasure as watching such Kansas All-Americans as Paul Endacott and Al Peterson.

This quiet, intelligent teacher died November 28, 1939, in Lawrence, Kansas, never fully realizing the popularity of the game he had invented.

2

BOB COUSY
Magician

Bob Cousy was a depressed young man. Here he had spent his college career in Worcester, Massachusetts, not far from Boston, had made All-American at Holy Cross, had played on a national championship team and had established a reputation as one of the best guards to play the game of college basketball.

Yet he would start his professional career basically as an "unwanted." The Boston Celtics could have selected him as a "territorial draft choice," but didn't, even though Bob had spoken often of his fondness for the Boston area and for playing with the Celtics.

The Celtics needed a big man at that time, however, and selected Chuck Share in the college draft. Bob Cousy went to a team called the Tri-Cities Hawks (a franchise which played in Moline and Rock Island, Illinois, plus Davenport, Iowa). "I had never even heard of Tri-Cities," Cousy said.

Luckily for Cousy, that was a period of transition and chaos in professional basketball. Many franchises folded and several players were shuttled around. Cousy was one. Tri-Cities actually had traded him for a guard

named Frank Brian. But the team Cousy was traded to
—the Chicago Stags—had folded and it was up to the
National Basketball Association to distribute the Stags'
players. The only other players on the Chicago roster
who had not been parceled out were a couple of stars,
Max Zaslofsky and Andy Phillip.

It was October 5, 1950 and the NBA owners were
closeted in the Sheraton Hotel in New York City.
Danny Biasone, the owner of the Syracuse franchise,
was anxious to get home so he offered his hat to Commissioner Maurice Podoloff and suggested a drawing.
Three numbers were placed in the hat. The New York
Knicks drew the first choice and selected Max Zaslofsky. The Philadelphia Warriors had the second selection and they chose Andy Phillip. That "left" the
Boston Celtics with Bob Cousy.

Cousy was as hesitant as the Celtics seemed to be. "I
felt the league was quite good and I had some doubts
about my making it," the 6-foot-1 Cousy said. "I was
thinking of entering some business when (Celtics owner Walter Brown) Mr. Brown called me, naming the
Celtics as my pro club."

Bob Cousy, of course, did join the Celtics and
played for 13 years in the NBA. During that time, he
solidified his reputation as the best little man to play
the game and he became one of the most spectacular
figures in basketball history, proving that there always
will be a place for the clever backcourt man.

Cousy made basketball fun for thousands of fans
who turned out all over the country to watch him
guide one of the greatest dynasties in the history of
sports. Put a ball in Cousy's hands and one could not
anticipate the next move. It might go behind his back,
between his legs, over his head. Nobody, especially
the defense, knew. His strong point was playmaking,
but he was an excellent scorer, too.

From 1952 through 1960, Cousy led the National Basketball Association in assists. And when he retired at the the end of the 1963 season, he left behind an incredible set of statistics and memories. He once held the all-time league record for minutes played (30,230) and he also held the record for assists (6,949) including the single game mark of 28 set against the Lakers in 1959. When he retired he was the fourth leading scorer in league history with 16,955 points and was second in total games played (917). For 10 years he was named to the league's all-star team. And he was the only player to participate in 13 all-star games.

In 1962, a poll of sports editors of 100 major daily papers named Cousy the NBA's all-time top player. There weren't many arguments. "I've seen many great ones since I began fooling around with a ball in 1912," said Joe Lapchick, who coached the Knicks when Cousy was with Boston. "I've seen Johnny Beckman, Nat Holman, Hank Luisetti, Bob Davies, George Mikan, the best of the big men, to name just a few.

"Bob Cousy," Lapchick continued, "is the best I've ever seen. He does so many things. It's so hard to say that Cousy can think in the air or that Cousy does this or that. Cousy does everything. He's regularly one of the league's top scorers. When a guy's a scorer, you usually don't expect him to be a leader in the other departments. One talent generally suffers from another. Bob, however, has been a leader in assists . . . and he's become a very capable defensive player and a tremendous pass stealer.

"I was just thinking of games we've played against Cousy. He always shows you something new, something you've never seen before. Any mistake against him and you pay the full price. One step and he's past the defense. He's quick, he's smart, he's tireless, he has spirit and he is probably the best finisher in sports."

Robert Joseph Cousy was born August 9, 1928, in the Yorkville section of New York City. Six months earlier, his parents had arrived from France. When Bob was 11, the family moved from Manhattan's upper East Side to St. Albans in suburban Queens County.

The youngster played a lot of baseball, but basketball soon became his favorite. He made the varsity at Andrew Jackson High School in Queens during his junior year and scored 28 points in his first game. At the end of his high school career he had made New York City's highly-regarded all-scholastic team, and he went on to Holy Cross College. His first coach at Holy Cross was Alvin (Doggie) Julian and later he played for Lester (Bubb) Sheary. Those were great years at Holy Cross with Cousy joining such excellent players as Joe Mullaney, Dermie O'Connell, George Kaftan, Frank Oftring and Bob McMullan.

Sheary always badgered Cousy about using his left hand, explaining that it would make him a better ball-handler and player. If Cousy opened a car door with his right hand, Sheary would tell him about it. "You need a better left hand," Sheary repeated. "They're overplaying your right side. Everybody knows you're going to shoot with the right hand. Do me a favor please. Open doors with your left hand. Carry books with your left hand . . . and come up to the gym and work on your left hand." Cousy did. Hour after hour. And from that hard work came the ball-handling ability that would manifest itself so spectacularly later in his career. "We never had a big man," Cousy explained about his Holy Cross days, "so we developed 101 variations on the give and go.

"They claim we sold basketball to New England, but we may have also retarded it. Possibly we oriented the people in the wrong direction by emphasizing the spectacular."

Later, during his professional career, Cousy claimed that his fancy ball-handling maneuvers, such as behind-the-back passes, had been exaggerated in proportion to the rest of his game. "Actually," he said, "I don't use the behind-the-back pass as often as people think I do. When I use it, I have a good reason for it. When a situation develops where I can help the club with a certain maneuver, I go ahead with it."

He added, "I think what's helped me more than anything is that I get a much bigger kick out of setting up a play than scoring a basket. As a result, I've done a lot of experimenting in keeping control of the ball, mostly in the heat of a game. I've learned to dribble, pass and transfer the ball from hand to hand behind my back.

"But I never pull those stunts unless I have to. I'll do something behind my back when I'm too well covered to do it the conventional way. My faking is no different from anyone else's. All good pros can fake. I may get away with it more often because of my physical attributes. I have long arms and big hands and good peripheral vision, so sometimes I can work a little faster and see a little more without turning my head."

Cousy's explanations didn't stop his Boston Teammates from forming their own ideas about his style and what that style meant to the Celtics. "What amazes me is Bob's ability to respond to sudden situations," said Bill Sharman, who played the backcourt with Cousy through many of the Boston golden years.

"One time on a fast-break, Bob started to go behind his back as a defender lunged at him near the Celtics basket," Sharman remembered. "Bob had started to switch the ball from his right hand to his left, but the fellow suddenly fell back. Cousy, instead of completing the behind-the-back movement, quickly slapped the ball to the floor with his right hand, continued the dribble and went in unmolested for the basket. I never saw any faster thinking and movement."

Through the years, Cousy had some exciting duels with a number of opposing professional players like Slater Martin of the Lakers and later the Hawks; Larry Costello of Philadelphia and Dick McGuire of the Detroit Pistons and New York Knicks. "Covering Cousy's dribble," McGuire said, "is like trying to catch a yo-yo."

"He makes the Celtics go," Martin added. "He's the greatest. I get more of a boot out of holding him down than scoring myself." Jack George, a backcourt man who played for Philadelphia and New York, had many frustrating moments against Cousy. "You can never tell which way he is going with the ball. He had men to hit with his passes and yet he was poppin' 'em from the outside," George said.

Night after night, year after year it was the same. The assists, the scoring, the Celtic wins and the Celtic championships. Late in his career, Cousy admitted "The joy went out a long time ago. By the middle of the season I'm sick and tired of basketball." But how, then, does a professional continually keep a mental edge that allows him to play great basketball night after night as Cousy did throughout his career even when the opposition was so intent on stopping him?

"You can play a decent game without being up," Cousy admitted. "But I wait for the game to start and I look for external things to get me up."

"It's that way all the time," Cousy said about the pressure the defenses continually put on him. "They come out of the locker room all fired up. But I find they can't sustain that concentration all game long. I just pace myself in the first half. Statistics will show that I do 65 to 75 per cent of my scoring in the second half . . . They can't resist going all out right away. They figure if they can shut me off the first half, I'll get tired or discouraged . . . I try to add something. The last couple of years I've been working on a running one-hander off either foot that's pulled the defense out.

". . . What I try to do is pick an incident or think of some personal rivalry as a means of getting myself worked up for a given game . . . If we're playing St. Louis, I recall all the times Slater Martin has out-smarted me and I say to myself, 'This time I'll show I'm better than he is.' "

Cousy had to endure the defensive pressure night after night and he was thankful for the 24-second rule adopted by the NBA during the 1954–55 season. "It's been a boon to me," Cousy said. "Especially in the last moments of a game when I'm trying to protect the dribble in delaying tactics. In the days before the adoption of the 24-second rule, brother, I used to get mauled trying to hang on to the ball. I went to the foul line often, and I wonder whether it was worth the beating I used to take . . . but I can't blame my opponents. They had to try and get possession."

But Cousy the magician wasn't only respected on the court by the players around the league. They also benefited from the fact that he was one of those mainly responsible for starting the NBA Players' Association which today is a powerful force in player-management relations.

When Cousy announced his retirement in 1963 to accept a head coaching job at Boston College, the fans around the league and the teams he played against made a number of emotional farewells. But nothing was more emotional than Bob Cousy's farewell to Boston. "This is the finest thing that has ever happened to me," Cousy told 13,909 Boston Garden fans who honored him with a special day March 17, 1963. He spoke the words with deep feeling in the huge, hushed arena.

President Kennedy sent a telegram, many of his ex-teammates flew in from all over the country for the event. The Mayor of Boston cried. Celtics' coach Red Auerbach embraced him at mid-court. "Imagine," Auerbach said, "how I feel losing a guy like Cousy . . . He's the closest thing to perfection."

And so Bob Cousy went off to coach college basketball. And from there he moved back to the professional game as coach of the Cincinnati Royals where, out of desperation, he played briefly for seven games during the 1969–70 season.

Of course, the old skills and moves were gone after the six-year layoff, but that brief return brought back a fading era when the Boston Celtics were the greatest team in sports and Bob Cousy was the man bringing the ball up for Bill Russell and Tom Heinsohn or setting up Bill Sharman.

"I think we had the greatest basketball team that's ever been put together, led by the shrewdest coach, operated by the most generous owner and playing in the best city before the fairest fans," Cousy said. "If that sounds like pouring it on, I'm sorry. But I mean every word of it."

BASKETBALL'S HALL OF FAME

3

GEORGE MIKAN
Giant of the Half-Century

First it was the coach at Joliet, Illinois, Catholic High School. He was delivering a pep talk to the youngsters on the basketball team. As the coach talked, he noticed George Mikan squinting at him. "George," the coach said, "I'm afraid you need glasses and I never heard of any basketball player with glasses ever amounting to anything. I'm sorry, but I'll have to cut you from the squad."

Next it was George Keogan, the coach at Notre Dame, who told George Mikan he didn't have the talent. "He's too awkward," Keogan said, "and he wears glasses." George Mikan did wear glasses, with lenses a quarter of an inch thick. But by the middle of the 1950s few people in basketball noticed.

George Mikan revolutionized the game of basketball. He was the first of the great big men. He could shoot and score and rebound and, even more surprising, could handle the ball exceptionally well. In 1949, Joe Lapchick, the Hall of Famer who played for the Original Celtics and later coached the New York Knickerbockers, said, "George Mikan is the greatest all-around basketball player that ever lived and the highest-paid and the greatest gate attraction. He's the Ruth, the Dempsey, the Hagen, the Tilden, of basketball. And one swell fellow along with it."

It was an accurate summation. Everyone—except for the 48 minutes they spent playing against him— liked the 6-foot-10 graduate of De Paul. He was an intelligent and talented man who earned a law degree, was an accomplished pianist and a candidate for the United States Congress. Mikan later became the first commissioner of the American Basketball Association.

His ABA role was ironic because Mikan was the person most responsible for making the National Basketball Association a successful league. Mikan was the center for one of the greatest teams in the history of professional basketball—the Minneapolis Lakers of the late 1940s and early 1950s. The team won six championships in seven years in the National Basektball League and later the NBA. "I will say it was the greatest team in the history of basketball and deserves a place not earned by any team in any other type of athletics. The Lakers have been the greatest contributing factor to the success of the NBA," said commissioner Maurice Podoloff.

And George Mikan was the greatest contributing factor to the success of the Lakers. He became the Basketball Player of the Half-Century as chosen by the Associated Press.

He did it because he was a worker. He survived a near-crippling leg injury when he was a youngster, and then survived his own awkwardness. It was Ray Meyer, the coach at De Paul, whose patience and help transformed Mikan into one of the game's leading scorers.

"Ray," Mikan said when he was at De Paul, "stresses coordination and insists a man can never be a star unless he wants to be. So I've worked out every day and have even skipped rope, punched the bag and sparred in order to develop the coordination he demands.

"At De Paul my first year (1942) I was a freak. I was like the fat lady in the circus, or the tattoed man. I was big and I was alive, I could get the ball on the jump, but of what other use could I be? I would stand under the basket and just reach out for the ball if it came off the backboard in my direction. But I was really regarded by the fans like that midget Bill Veeck used when he had the St. Louis Browns. So I worked on the hook shot. The hook shot was what started them —the opposition—thinking.

"Ray was a slave-driver. But he was just what I needed. He taught me everything I know. In fact, it hardly seems possible that I've learned so much in three short years."

Meyer was not bashful when it came to evaluating Mikan's talent. "If (Bill) Russell and Mikan were playing opposite one another today (1956)," he said, "I would have to rate Mikan a better player. I am not saying this because Mikan once played for me. For example, if Mikan and Russell went up for a jump ball —and both players stand about 6-10—Mikan would shove Russell aside because of his superior weight and get the tip. Mikan is a brute. When Mikan wanted to be rough, he could do it. That is why he drew so many fouls."

The 245-pound Mikan worked and worked and made All-America three straight years. He led the major colleges in scoring in 1945 (23.9) and 1946 (23.1). His greatest collegiate achievment was a 120-point three game performance which enabled De Paul to win the 1945 National Invitation Tournament title.

His greatest game came in a semifinal during that tournament. It was against Rhode Island State. The day before the game, Mikan, weary and fighting a number of minor injuries, spent most of his time in bed, resting. It had been a brutal season. Everywhere he played, he was double- and triple-teamed, and he often absorbed tremendous physical punishment.

It was no different against Rhode Island. Anytime he stationed himself in his pivot position, he found three players surrounding him. They mauled and pushed and chopped at his arms, but it didn't stop him. Mikan scored 53 points to set a Madison Square Garden record. What made the performance even more incredible was the fact that Mikan scored as many points as the whole Rhode Island team. The score was 97–53. Years later, players like Wilt Chamberlain and Lew Alcindor made 53-point performances commonplace, but when Mikan was playing very few players averaged even 20 points per game.

In 1946, George Mikan signed a five-year $60,000 contract with the Chicago Gears of the National Basketball League. In his first pro game, he learned what his career would be like. The Gears were playing the team from Oshkosh, Wisconsin, and the Wisconsin team had a center named Cowboy Edwards, who was to guard Mikan. One of Edwards' first moves was to knock out four of Mikan's teeth. Mikan averaged 16.5 points per game that first year.

Then at the start of the 1947–48 season, the Chicago team folded and its players were distributed among the other teams in the league. George Mikan went to Minneapolis, where he remained seven seasons before retiring with virtually every scoring record in professional basketball.

He led the NBL in scoring in the 1947–48 season with 1,195 points, then when the Lakers switched to the NBA, he led that league in scoring three straight seasons (1948–49 through 1950–51). He had a lifetime NBA average of 23.1 points per game and was selected on the NBA All-Star first team six consecutive seasons.

To curb Mikan, the NBA passed a rule doubling the foul lane from 6 to 12 feet. The thought behind the move was to restrict Mikan where he was most powerful—close to the basket. The rulesmakers were wrong. It didn't stop him.

"Minneapolis screamed loudest when the 12-foot rule went in, but I insisted from the start that the widening of the foul lane would have no affect on the genuine stars," Joe Lapchick said at the time. "It's my opinion that it has made Mikan an even better basketball player. No longer can he plant himself under the basket and use his size, weight and elbows to advantage. He has to maneuver more and he maneuvers beautifully."

Mikan had many great moments in professional basketball, but his most memorable was his scoring surge at the end of the 1948–49 season, when he astounded the athletic world with performances of 48 points against New York, 53 against Baltimore, 51 against New York again and 46 against Rochester, all within the space of a few weeks.

His highest single game was 61 against the Royals in 1951–52, the same year that an irate fan threw a pocketknife at him from the stands in Rochester.

Because of his size, Mikan made an excellent target —for fans and players alike. During his career, from high school through professional ball, he suffered two broken legs. He also had broken bones in his right foot, the arch of his left foot, his right wrist, his nose and thumb. Three other fingers were broken and his nose was ripped open twice. All in all, doctors took 166 stitches.

Once, after a particularly difficult game in New

York, a reporter entered the Laker dressing room. The Knicks had accused Mikan of roughhouse tactics. He asked Mikan about it. Mikan looked at the reporter, pulled off his powder-blue road uniform with the famous number 99, and told the reporter to look at the black and blue marks on his chest, arms and back. "Ask them [the Knicks] what they think these are," Mikan said. "Birthmarks?"

"Nobody," said Mikan's Minneapolis teammate Jim Pollard, "gave George anything. He earned his baskets and he also got about 15 rebounds a game. Once he stationed himself under the basket, he was tough to push out. For rival players it must have been something like trying to move the Statue of Liberty. He'd have given Russell and Chamberlain some trouble."

Larry Foust of the Fort Wayne Pistons spent many frustrating afternoons and evenings trying to stop Mikan. "I competed against George for almost seven years and I've got the elbow marks to prove it," Foust said. "Mikan ran the whole show. He was an athlete despite what some people say about his bulk, and nobody ever had better offensive moves under the basket. When George played, he owned that lane. And I'd have to feel he'd own it if he played today. Russell and Chamberlain? Well, they're wonderful. But Mikan was better."

Foust was a player trying to stop Mikan. Lapchick, who coached New York, had to think of strategic things to tell his players about curtailing Mikan's efforts. "I shudder to think what he might have done under the old rules," Lapchick said. "If he had been playing back in the old days when I was with the Celtics, he'd have scored a million. We've tried every known defense on him and nothing works. Sure we can stop him by covering him with three men, but then Jim Pollard, Vern Mikkelsen and the other Lakers score like crazy. What have you gained? Nothing. In fact, you've lost more than you've gained."

Mikan was often asked to compare the Laker teams he played for with the Boston Celtics, whose dynasty from 1958–59 through 1965–66 has been acclaimed the greatest in basketball. "Naturally," Mikan said, "I lean toward the Lakers. Actually it's a question no one really can answer. It's like trying to compare the 1927 Yankees with the Yankees in their modern heyday. But I think the Lakers would have done all right against the Celtics. In fact, they would have done all right against any team—in any era.

"Maybe we didn't quite have Boston's depth, but we had everything else. People forget that most of us played at least three years under the 24-second rule. We could do a few things and we could also win on the road. I think I could have scored against Russell and Chamberlain because I was always careful to turn tight on rival centers and throw the ball off my shoulder. If you extend your arm to its full length, naturally fellows like Bill and Wilt are going to block your shot.

"Most of the boys had their own pet pivot tricks. Some tried bullying and threatening me. That was all right with me. When they played rough, I played rough. I was capable of taking care of myself in the clinches."

At the end of the 1953–54 season, when he was thirty, Mikan announced his retirement as an active player. He would become the general manager of the Lakers and would open his law practice.

"This," said Laker coach John Kundla, "should even up the league." It did exactly that. It also nearly ruined attendance in Minneapolis. By January 1956, the Lakers were desperate. Then one cold winter day, Mikan called a press conference. The general manager would become an active player again.

The comeback was not easy. Out of shape, minus his timing, Mikan could not regain his old form. He played 37 games for the Lakers and averaged only 10.5 points per game. At the end of the season, he retired again—this time for good.

He went back to his law practice and then as a Republican candidate tried unsuccessfully for the congressional seat from the third district in Minnesota. "I never stop trying to make the best that I can of myself," he said. "I think I can be of some help to the people. My legal training got me interested in politics. I don't pretend to know the answers to all the problems. But I want to get out and talk to the people about them.

"I'm sincere about it," he continued. "I've gotten a fair shake in everything I've done and I'd like to help the others get the same thing."

Mikan lost the election to Roy Wier, the Democrat, 112,700 to 98,834. It was one of the few losses of his life. For in basketball, he was one of the game's greatest winners.

4

NAT HOLMAN
Mr. Basketball

The postal employees in New York City weren't
baffled for a moment. The letter didn't have the precise
information required, but it had enough.

It was from Manila and it was addressed in this
way:

> Mr. Basketball
> City College
> New York

Nat Holman's fans and disciples were everywhere—
on Twenty-third Street in mid-Manhattan as well as in
the Philippines. James Naismith invented the game,
George Mikan scored a lot of points, Adolph Rupp was
the winningest collegiate coach, but Nat Holman, well,
he was Mr. Basketball. Why? There were a number of
reasons.

He was the first genuine high scorer in the game
and was considered one of the smartest and most
rounded players when he was with the Original Celtics
in the 1920s. Later, as a coach, he made City College

of New York one of the most feared teams in the country, and he became the first man to direct a team to both the National Collegiate championship and the National Invitation Tournament title in one season.

Nat Holman was a New Yorker who grew up on the streets of the lower East Side. The Holmans were a big family, consisting of mother and father and ten children. Basketball in those days was very much a New York game, and Holman mastered it very quickly. Before he was twenty, he was one of the game's biggest names.

"Kid" Holman they called him in those days when he was performing wondrous deeds for Commerce High School in Manhattan. He could have moved in any athletic direction.

In football he was the All-Star left halfback on the Commerce team; he made the soccer team too and became the all-scholastic goalie; in baseball, he starred as a pitcher and second baseman for a team that lost the city championship by one game.

One weekend during the fall of 1915 he starred in a Friday afternoon soccer game, then followed that up the next day with a 50-yard run off tackle for Commerce's only score in a football game. That night he put his basketball shoes on and sparked the Henry St. Settlement House to one of its many victories.

When he was ready to graduate from high school, the Cincinnati Reds offered Holman a baseball contract. He refused it and instead enrolled in the Savage School of Physical Education, financing his education at Savage by playing professional basketball.

When Holman was twelve, he had earned a reputation as a fine basketball player. He obtained the reputation the hard way—playing in the rough neighborhood games against men much older and bigger than himself. Those were the days of the Henry St. Settlement House and later the Ninety-second Street YMHA team. Lack of years and lack of size never seemed to hamper Holman.

He steadily improved as a player and there was no doubt that he would become one of the great professionals. In 1917 and 1918 he played for Newark and for the first New York team to have the nickname "Knickerbockers." After serving with the U.S. Navy in World War I, Holman resumed his professional career playing with teams in Bridgeport, Connecticut, Germantown and Scranton, Pennsylvania, and for the Whirlwinds of New York City.

Like many of the "first generation" professionals, Holman found himself playing four and five nights a week and riding trains all night to get from one city to another. He remained on that schedule even when he was appointed head basketball coach at CCNY in 1919.

He would conduct practice, then jump on a train, hoping that nothing on the line prevented him from reaching that night's game on time. Once he was in such a hurry that he boarded the wrong train and wound up in Syracuse rather than Buffalo, where his team was playing. It was a tribute to the man that he worked at becoming the game's best player and best coach at the same time, never sacrificing one at the expense of the other.

Holman reached the top as a player with the Original Celtics, joining them for the 1921–22 season. He later became captain of the team that won 720 games out of the 795 they played between 1921 and 1928, when Holman was the star.

"Nat," said Joe Lapchick, his teammate, "was gifted in all phases of the game." It was an encompassing but apt description. Holman was considered the finest passer and playmaker of the era and, until Bob Cousy came along many years later, nobody came close to matching Nat's ability as ballhandler and backcourt man.

He also was an artist at the fake and feint, which made it extremely difficult for the opposition to guard and control him. In an era when teams seldom scored more than 30 points in one game, Holman was the high scorer for the Celtics, averaging 10 a game, the first player of national renown to own a double-figure average.

Holman was only 5-11, 165 pounds, and often he was on the receiving end of some very aggressive defensive maneuvers. His "protector" was the Celtics' center, Horse Haggerty. Many years later, after their success had forced the American Basketball League to order the Celtics' breakup, Holman wound up playing for Chicago and Haggerty for Washington.

The late George Preston Marshall, famed owner of the football Redskins, owned the Washington basketball team, too. He was an excitable man. One night, Chicago and Washington were involved in a game that was tied going into the final seconds. Haggerty had the ball for Washington when suddenly he heard a familiar voice call for it.

It was Holman, and Haggerty, acting on reflex, threw the ball to his ex-teammate, who then made the winning basket. On the Washington bench, Marshall picked up the water bucket and threw it high in the air.

Holman was a national hero in the 1920s. Wherever the Celtics performed, he was the drawing attraction. His was the role of the clean-cut hero who didn't smoke and took a glass of beer only when his weight started to decrease.

"Pride," Holman said, referring to his days with the Celtics. "Pride in ourselves. The stories you read about champions getting weary of winning are so much nonsense. No champion ever wins so many contests that he doesn't mind losing one."

All during these years, Holman steadily turned out winning teams at CCNY. "City," as it was known around New York, offered a free education to students from the five boroughs. The scholastic qualifications were high and there were no scholarships offered. The big stars went to other schools. Holman took the leftovers.

But he had one advantage: himself. He was a tremendous teacher whose devotion to detail was often overwhelming. He was a stubborn man, too. He believed in Eastern basketball and the patient, deliberate Eastern style of play. To Holman, the five most important ingredients in the game were ballhandling, shiftiness, endurance, shooting ability and poise.

His teams seldom were built around one player and it was rare when one man dominated play. This didn't mean CCNY was devoid of stars. There were plenty, such people as Tubby Raskin, Bernie Schiffer, Mac Hodesblatt, Ace Goldstein, Moe Goldman, Red Phillips, Sid Trubowitz, Bernie Fliegel, Red Holzman, Irwin Dambrot, Lionel Malamed, Ed Warner, Floyd Layne and Ed Roman.

During his thirty-six seasons at CCNY, Holman's teams won 421 games and lost 188. And though he didn't agree at first with the Western style of play, which featured the fast break and the one-hand shot, Holman later reconsidered and installed it in his program, his players mastering the best of the new style as well as the best of the old. The combination added up to many of the 421 victories.

City's teams operated with very few set plays. "I want resourceful, flexible-thinking teams that are never stuck for an idea on what to do next," Holman said. "I teach my players to recognize situations and know what will develop from a particular floor pattern. . . . All basketball is a pattern. Get in that pattern and then you're going."

His players knew how to play all four corners of the court and the middle, too. They all had to be able to score from outside the foul circle. There was no excessive dribbling, and fancy passes were out.

The greatest moment of his coaching career came at the end of the 1949–50 season, when the Beavers swept to the NCAA and NIT crowns for the first time in history. The basketball world was astounded. It had been the greatest single feat in the collegiate game.

He had some outstanding individuals, but their individuality never became dominant. The team was the important thing. The center on that CCNY team was Ed Roman, who at 6-6 was the tallest player Holman had coached in thirty-two years. Ed Warner was the closest the Beavers came to having a star. Only 6-2, Warner had been blessed with extraordinary jumping ability. He often went into the pivot when Roman was out of the lineup. Al Roth, a set-shot artist, and Floyd Layne, a hard driver, were the backcourt men. Irwin Dambrot, a 6-4 forward, was the fifth man. His forte was rebounding and ballhandling.

Roman, Warner, Roth and Layne were sophomores. Dambrot and sixth-man Norm Mager were seniors. Despite the presence of four inexperienced players, CCNY finished with a 17–5 record during the regular season.

The NIT, searching for its final entry, decided on the local team, and CCNY was in but unseeded. The Beavers' first game was against the defending NIT champion, San Francisco. The Dons were heavily favored to end CCNY's season promptly.

But it never happened, and with that game CCNY started a streak of upset victories that eventually captivated a basketball-conscious nation. The Beavers beat

San Francisco, 65–46, then followed with an unbelievable 89–50 victory over the University of Kentucky, which had won the national championship the year before. For the second straight night, Warner scored 26 points.

A 62–52 victory over Duquesne put Holman's team in the finals against Bradley, and again they were the underdogs. By now interest in CCNY had spread from one end of the country to the other. Could the Beavers do it? Could the unseeded last choice win the coveted NIT title? Bradley was 26–3, and the Braves played like it, jumping to an 11-point lead. CCNY slowly cut it down, eventually went ahead and finally won, 69–61.

City, despite its NIT victory, was the last team invited to the NCAA tournament. Again, the Beavers were expected to exit quickly.

Maybe the newspapermen and the experts thought that way, but the fans were beginning to realize this was a special team, one that couldn't be judged by won-lost records.

Ohio State was the first opponent—and victim—in the NCAA. It wasn't easy, however, CCNY eking out a 56–55 victory. That moved the team into the Eastern finals against North Carolina State, another team favored to eliminate the Beavers. This time CCNY controlled the game and won, 78–73, to set up a rematch with Bradley in the finals. Had CCNY's victory the weekend before been a fluke? The Beavers answered by making it two in a row over the Braves, 71–68, and for the first time in history a team had won both college titles in one season.

Holman was now the king of collegiate basketball, but the euphoria ended abruptly the next season. Not because CCNY lacked talent, but because its players were implicated in a point-shaving scandal that ended the school's days as a major power. The scandals, however, could not erase the accomplishments of the 1949–50 team. Holman was the first to realize this.

"They gave me my greatest thrill," Holman said. "They were playing basketball during those tournaments and they were still a team. I've always tried to teach team play. I don't think I'd care to have the country's leading scorer. I'd be too worried about how many shots he was taking.

"But anyway, for that grand-slam period these kids were a real team. Afterwards, well, I don't like to talk about the scandals. They stir too many memories. When they won those two tournaments they poured out their best and personified my theories. Then . . . they let me down."

The explosion came about a year after CCNY won the two championships. The Beavers had just crushed Temple in Philadelphia's Palestra and were on the train returning to New York. Some New York detectives also were aboard and they told Holman their reason for being there. Seven CCNY players later became implicated in the point-shaving scandals.

Holman received much criticism. The college, charging that he had been lax in supervising his players, suspended him. Holman appealed. It was a nasty, sticky mess, but Holman refused to give in. Yes, CCNY had contributed to the overemphasis of college basketball in New York, but did that suddenly mean he was not fit to teach?

Finally, he was reinstated. It had been a long, drawn-out battle, but now CCNY no longer was a power. Holman would be coaching a very ordinary basketball team. It didn't matter to him. He was back in the game he loved. "When I came back in 1954," he remembered, "we were playing Adelphi. The fans gave me a standing ovation. I'll never forget it."

Holman continued to coach at CCNY until September 1, 1960, when he announced his retirement due to health problems.

A few weeks later, in the Hotel Manhattan, Nat Holman sat on the dais at his testimonal dinner and looked out at four hundred of his friends sitting in the packed dining room.

There were the surviving members of the Celtics— Joe Lapchick, Pete Barry, Dutch Dehnert. There were former CCNY players, opposing collegiate coaches; Dr. Buell Gallagher, the CCNY president who suspended Holman, also was in the audience.

Fifty years of the game's history sat in that room and honored the man who, wrote Gene Roswell in the New York *Post,* "made the bounce of a basketball synonymous with the heartbeat of a great, teeming public college."

Holman did that, but he did much more for basketball over the years. He was its first superstar, then one of its great coaching figures. More important, though, he was a pioneer, spreading the game's gospel in the days when it had few salesmen. He never stopped selling it, even after his official retirement. The game was too much a part of him and he was too much a part of the game.

5

HANK LUISETTI
Big Shot from the West

The powerful lights of Madison Square Garden cut through the silvery blue cigarette haze, illuminating the basketball court for a game that eventually would revolutionize a sport. It was December 30, 1936, and Long Island University, winner of 43 straight games, would meet Stanford, the team from the West Coast.

What little was known about Stanford came from newspaper clippings. The Indians had a great scorer named Hank Luisetti, and they had a fine record, but West Coast teams had played in the Garden before and flopped badly. Why, New Yorkers asked, should this team be any different?

It was an historic meeting, this contest between a team that relied on the deliberate, old-fashioned Eastern style of play and the new run-and-shoot Western game. And the man who transformed Stanford, and then basketball, was Angelo (Hank) Luisetti, who introduced the one-hand push shot to the East.

This bit of history may sound strange in the modern era of running jump shots and scores of 125–120. But until Luisetti, basketball shooting was a relatively simple thing. From the outside, a player shot with two hands. From the inside he either worked for the conventional layup or positioned himself for a hook shot.

Easterners had heard that Luisetti would show them something different in Madison Square Garden. Nat Holman, the coach at City College, seemed indignant that someone would try a new shot.

"I'll quit coaching," he said, "if I have to teach one-handed shots to win. They'll have to show me plenty to convince me that a shot predicated on a prayer is smart basketball. There's only one way to shoot, and that's the way we do it in the East—with two hands."

Two days before its game in New York, Stanford defeated a strong Temple team in Philadelphia, 45–38. In New York the fans began to sense something important might happen in the game between the Indians and LIU.

A crowd of 17,623 packed the Garden for the game. LIU was the solid favorite. It was a team with such collegiate stars as Julie Bender, Art Hillhouse and Ben Kramer. At the 11-minute mark the score was tied at 11–11. Then Luisetti sparked Stanford to a 19–11 lead. His one-handed shots were accurate, his dribbling deceptive, his passing sharp and accurate, his rebounding solid and his defensive play in the Stanford zone excellent.

With three minutes left in the game, Stanford had a safe lead, thanks to Luisetti, who had scored 15 points, high for those days. He also had played one of the finest all-around games in the history of Madison Square Garden. When he walked off the floor, he received a standing ovation from the crowd. The final score was 45–31, the first time LIU had been beaten in three years.

"I'll never forget the look on Art Hillhouse's face when I took that first shot," Luisetti said. "He was about 6-8 and he never expected a shot like that to be thrown. Guess he'd never seen one.

"When it hit I could just see him saying, 'Boy, is this guy lucky.' But that was the way we shot. That was what made it for us. Nobody but us believed we would win that night."

His one-handed shot had captivated the audience and the press. The next morning *The New York Times* carried this report: "It seemed Luisetti could do nothing wrong. Some of his shots would have been deemed foolhardy if attempted by anybody else, but with Luisetti shooting, these were accepted by the enchanted crowd."

Shortly thereafter, kids in New York, Philadelphia, Washington, Detroit, kids in Iowa, kids in Kansas, kids everywhere, were shooting running one-handers like Hank Luisetti.

"I guess we didn't really know what we were starting that night," Luisetti said. "We actually had no idea that we would bring on a revolution. You know, I've thought about that night many times over the years. I had no notion what that one game would mean to me.

"Getting all that publicity in New York changed my life, my whole life. It made me a national figure with stories about me in the *Saturday Evening Post* and *Collier's* and all that. I had just been a local kid up to then."

Hank Luisetti was one of the most versatile players in the history of basketball. Some even contend he was the best performer in the sport. "I can't remember anybody who could do more things," said Clair Bee, the LIU coach. "He was an amazing marksman, a spectacular dribbler and awfully clever passer," said Holman. Joe Lapchick, the St. John's coach, said, "The thing I remember about him was his uncanny ability to control the ball while going at top speed."

Luisetti was born June 16, 1916, in the Telegraph Hill section of San Francisco. His neighborhood produced some other pretty fair athletes like Joe DiMaggio, Tony Lazzeri and Frank Crosetti. Luisetti's father was a chef.

When he was six, young Hank began shooting baskets. At Galileo High School he began to develop the one-handed shot. "I don't know how I came to think of it," he said. "It just seemed to be the natural way to get the ball in the air."

His high school coach, Tommy Denike, didn't try to stop him. "I let him do it," Denike said, "because the ball seemed to drop in the basket more often than not. Boy, wouldn't I have felt funny if I had tried to change his style."

The black-haired, dark-eyed youngster moved on to Stanford, where he perfected his famed shot. "If a guy can putt standing on his head," Luisetti said, "he's a good putter. When I was a freshman I asked coach Johnny Bunn if I could stay with the one-hander even though the coaches of those days died when you tried it. I was standing near the corner during practice and I popped one in. Bunn said quietly, 'Stay with it, boy.'"

The season was 1934–35, and Luisetti's freshman team was undefeated. The 6-3 forward scored 305 points in eighteen games. The next year his point total jumped to 416, then 410 and 465 for a collegiate total of 1,596. His average for three seasons was 16.5 points per game, and his reward was a position on the All-American team each season.

Luisetti was an extremely unselfish player, so unselfish, in fact, that his teammates decided to conspire against him in one game during the 1937–38 season. The opponent that night was Duquesne, the powerful team from Pittsburgh. The game was played on a neutral court in Cleveland, Ohio. His teammates always felt that Luisetti didn't shoot enough. He was a fine passer who would rather make sure of a percentage shot than take one from the outside himself. His teammates, however, thought the "percentage" shot was the one that Hank took.

On this particular night against Duquesne, Luisetti started playing his normal game. His passing, as usual, was excellent. But every time he passed to his team-mates, they passed the ball right back to him, forcing him to shoot. He set a record 50 points that night as the Indians defeated the Dukes, 92–27.

Coach Bunn couldn't help praising him. "He was not only the greatest player I ever had," Bunn said, "but he also is one of the finest men I've ever known. Those were great clubs to coach. Every regular was a crack player who could score, pass and run. The only way they could have stopped Luisetti would have been to put a lid on the basket. No mere commonplace defense ever could keep him from scoring.

"He was a dream player. Once I remember he missed 6 foul shots in a row. He came rushing over to the bench. 'Take me out, Coach,' he said. 'I'm terrible.' So I took him out and gave him a rest for a few minutes. Then he went back in. Oh, yes, he managed to pop in 10 before the game ended. And that was on a bad day.

"They used to ask me how I felt about coaching the best basketball player of the age. Well, my answer was always the same: I always said that Hank Luisetti is the young man who made a coach out of John Bunn. He could have made a coach out of anybody."

Luisetti was proud of his contributions to basket-ball. "I wasn't too bad a ballplayer," he said. "I had the whole game. I had flash, but I had more. I was all-around. I could shoot long, shoot short, drive, tip rebounds, play defense and in tough games I was a clutch player.

"That's when I rose. I laughed a lot, we all did, but inside I guess I had the killer instinct. Inside I was serious as hell. I would do well today. I'd do well any day. Maybe I wouldn't get as many tips with somebody like Wilt Chamberlain around because I wouldn't get in close, but I'd get my points."

Before the Luisetti era, Stanford had won only one Pacific Coast Conference title—in 1920. With Hank in the lineup, Stanford won three titles and was voted collegiate team of the year in 1936–37. Luisetti twice was named collegiate player of the year (1936–37, 1937–38).

After leaving Stanford, Luisetti was asked to make a movie in Hollywood about basketball. Betty Grable was the star and the movie was titled *Campus Confessions*. It was the first flop in Luisetti's life and it caused him a lot of problems.

The Amateur Athletic Union suspended him for a year because, it said, he had acted as a professional while making the movie. The AAU's ruling prohibited Luisetti from playing in the national tournament, then the premier event in basketball.

He was allowed to play in the tournament in 1940, however, and he set a tournament scoring record and was voted the outstanding player. He also proved he was still the game's biggest gate attraction. "Luisetti's presence," said an AAU spokesman, "added at least $5,000 to the gate."

The following year he joined the Phillips Oilers and injured his knee. Then came World War II. He enlisted in the Navy and was assigned to St. Mary's preflight. He played a lot of service basketball and averaged as astounding 30 points a game. In 1944 he was assigned to sea duty, but before he left he was hospitalized with spinal meningitis.

He recovered, but the illness had drained him and

the doctors told him he would be risking his health if he tried to play basketball again. It was a bitter disappointment to Luisetti, especially at that time, for modern professional basketball was emerging.

When news spread that Luisetti would not be able to play pro ball, a number of colleges asked him to take a coaching job. At first he didn't think it wise, because he didn't feel he had the best temperament for coaching. He did a little coaching, however, and he was as successful at it as he was on the court. He decided to coach in 1949 with the Stewart Chevrolet team in San Francisco. He drilled the team his way. "I would like to work with a team of agile, fast men who are fundamentalists and match that team against today's hot-shot shooters," he said.

By the 1950–51 season he had the team he wanted and Stewart captured the AAU championship. After that he devoted his coaching time to a series of highly successful clinics in the Bay Area. Three of his clinic players later captained college teams: Don Bragg of UCLA, and Ken Flower and Tony Psaltis of USC.

He remained with Stewart as a sales manager and never lost his interest in basketball. He often criticized the modern game, which, he thought, had forgotten the basic principles stressed in the old days. "A one-armed paperhanger could count on his fingers the players who depend on finesse and a thorough knowledge of the game to help their teams win," he said.

Yes, the game had changed since that cold December night in 1936 when Stanford came into Madison Garden to play LIU. "Maybe we didn't realize it at the time," Luisetti said, "but I think we did bring in the fast break, and though those guys back East didn't think we could do it, we showed that you can shoot with one hand."

6

NED IRISH
Boy Promoter

Legends seem to grow and flourish as the years pass,
new facts having been injected into the story, old facts
having been forgotten. The popular legend about Edward (Ned) Simmons Irish, the man who promoted
basketball into the nation's greatest spectator sport, is
that he conceived his idea while on assignment to cover
a Manhattan College basketball game.

When the young sportswriter arrived at the tiny
campus gymnasium, it was so crowded that he had to
crawl through a window to gain admittance. Squeez-
ing his way in, he ripped his best pair of trousers. Instead of seeing fiery sparks (or so the legend goes), Ned
Irish had another vision. He saw thousands of fans
lined up to buy tickets to college doubleheaders in
Madison Square Garden.

Actually, the idea of promoting college basketball in
Madison Square Garden was not a new one. The Mayor
of New York City, the colorful James J. (Jimmy)
Walker, desperate to help the relief funds during the
Depression, asked the sportswriters to promote some

benefit basketball games. Ned Irish was one of the writers who helped.

On January 19, 1931, a tripleheader packed the Garden. And on February 22, 1933, a seven-game program, which began in the afternoon and ran through the evening, drew 20,000.

Ned Irish was working as a sportswriter for the New York *World-Telegram* at a salary of $60 a week. As the Depression lingered, his salary grew slimmer and slimmer and finally dwindled to $48 a week.

Ned Irish had tremendous respect for the value of a dollar. His father had died when he was three and the family existed on his mother's meager salary as a dermatologist at Erasmus High School in Brooklyn and on whatever cash Ned brought in from odd jobs. He worked at a soda fountain during those days and then began covering schoolboy sports, receiving space-rate payments from the newspapers. Irish never minded the long hours and difficult work.

Nor was he afraid to take a gamble. Basketball in 1934 seemed to be a gamble to everyone but Irish. "Writing sports gave me a high opinion of college basketball," he said. "It seemed to me there was plenty of interest in the game which only needed development. I was convinced of it after I had helped promote two Garden tripleheaders for the Mayor's Unemployment Relief Fund in 1931."

Irish saw a great future for the game. But he also saw small, inadequate playing arenas hardly able to seat the many students who wanted to attend the games. The public, it seemed, was neglected and shut out.

"I realized and knew conditions, both in the local gymnasiums and in the armories, were very poor for the playing of basketball," Irish said. "The capacity of these places was inadequate; the lighting was poor.

"Only in the case of Fordham University was the

gymnasium nearly adequate to accommodate the attendance. As a result I contacted representatives of various local colleges with the proposition to play some of their games in Madison Square Garden."

There were ten colleges in the New York area alone that played top-flight basketball. New York University, a school with 7,500 students, had a gym with only 1,500 seats. Fordham's gym sat 2,500; City College, with an enrollment of 12,000, could handle only 1,200 at its games.

He figured that if he could import the top teams from around the country to New York to oppose these schools, he could fill the Garden, which at that time had a capacity of little more than 16,000.

So he went with a plan to General John Reed Kilpatrick, president of Madison Square Garden. Irish would guarantee the Garden $4,000 for use of the arena. Irish would handle the details, such as scheduling, tickets and publicity. If the gate exceeded the guarantee, Irish said, the Garden would receive a cut. Kilpatrick, whose building was dark too many nights a week, agreed.

On the night of December 29, 1934, Irish promoted his first doubleheader, matching St. John's and Westminster, and N.Y.U. and Notre Dame. A crowd of 16,138 saw the inaugural. It was a rather large birthday party for big-time college basketball. When the lights finally went out in the Garden that night, Irish had earned more money than he would have earned in six months with the *World-Telegram*. So it was goodbye, newspaper business.

From that point the game grew and grew. Irish grew with it. His theory about the students supporting the game proved correct. His other theory, that basketball was an excellent spectator sport, was also correct.

The idea was such a success that other people began

noticing. Soon Irish was being asked to promote games in Philadelphia, where his nucleus was Temple, St. Joseph's and Pennsylvania. He also promoted in Hershel, Pennsylvania, and Buffalo, N.Y. Everywhere he went, people praised him for his foresight. "Don't be silly," he answered. "The opportunity was always there. The thing that surprises me is that it waited for me to get around to it."

Irish learned about business early in life. When he was graduated from Erasmus High, he selected the University of Pennsylvania for his college education because no New York paper had a student correspondent at the Philadelphia school. Irish wasn't satisfied to cover Penn for six New York papers. He went out and signed four Philadelphia papers, too. The University of Pennsylvania was one of the best-covered teams in the East.

Much later in his career, the Garden came to realize that Irish was an extremely astute businessman. When he became president and a director of the Garden, he found himself in charge of labor relations—in addition to his other duties. That meant he had to deal with seventeen different labor unions whose men worked in the Garden.

Basketball was only the catalyst for his meteoric career as a promoter. He also was adept at other attractions: booking the circus, the rodeo, wrestling, some boxing, horse shows, track meets, dog shows, professional basketball, hockey plus his doubleheaders in the huge arena that was then between Forty-ninth and Fiftieth streets on Eighth Avenue.

Though he started as a newspaperman, Irish, a distant and aloof individual, alienated a great many reporters—and a great many others, too—with his harsh, businesslike attitude. "I don't care what they say about me, as long as they buy tickets," was one of his mottos.

Soon he became known as the "landlord" and "czar"

of college basketball, two descriptions which he greatly disliked. "Of course out-of-town teams communicate with me and I in turn am in a position to relay information, and, when asked, make suggestions. In other words, I act as sort of a clearing house," he said.

Then he added, "Madison Square Garden is not interested in controlling basketball throughout the country. It's too big a sport for that."

Basketball's growth was stunning—even to Irish, who realized the game's potential but did not realize it had quite the potential to sell out 20 of 21 programs during the 1945–46 season and attract more than 500,000 fans. The peak years for his doubleheaders were 1942 through 1949, with standing-room-only crowds jamming the Garden from 1946 through 1948.

The basketball scandal abruptly ended all that growth. It was 1951 and CCNY and LIU were among the best teams in the country. They were drawing huge throngs to the Garden, and then the news broke that some of the players on those teams as well as other teams around the city and country had shaved points. CCNY and LIU canceled the rest of their schedule and even dropped basketball for a few seasons. In New York the college game never recovered from that blow.

Irish received much criticism. Six years before the scandal broke he had appeared in court and testified that gambling was not a real problem in the Garden. But in a formal report after the scandal, New York District Attorney Frank Hogan claimed that gamblers in the Garden "were as obvious as giraffes." He accused Irish of knowing about the situation and doing nothing to correct it. "Underlying the scandal was the blatant commercialism which had permeated college basketball. What once had been a minor sport had been hippodromed into a big business," Hogan said.

Irish, a thin-lipped, balding man, remained his aloof

self. He refused to admit that he or the Garden was at fault. And the Garden went right on promoting double-headers the next year. Attendance, however, was not the same.

Except for the Holiday Festival during Christmas week and the National Invitation Tournament in March, the old excitement was gone. In the 1960s, crowds of 4,000 and 5,000 were common for double-headers involving the local schools.

Professional basketball, however, was successful, and Irish was a big factor in its growth. He was president of the New York Knickerbockers, a position of power and authority.

In the early days of the Basketball Association of America and later in the National Basketball Association, the New York franchise was the key because Garden money backed it. Irish let the owners know immediately that things would be run his way. He often infuriated some of the less wealthy owners with his threats to pull the New York franchise from the league when things didn't go his way.

"The way college basketball draws," he once said before the scandals, "the Knicks are nothing but a tax write-off anyway." That may have been true, but Irish and the Garden wanted a winner.

The team never won a championship, but in the early and mid 1950s was one of the strongest franchises in the league. Once again the fans were pouring through the admission gates. "I don't think the pros have taken the play away from the colleges," Irish said. "I think they've developed an entirely new following. Most places where the pros play there aren't major-college situations. Largely, the NBA is filling a vacuum that became evident as the sport developed, much as was the case with professional football.

"Ten to 15 percent of the pro fans were never interested in college basketball and never would be. They haven't got any particular college background."

Irish often was asked if the scandals led directly to the growth of the professional game. "I doubt," he replied, "that anybody who was interested in basketball at that time will ever forget it, but I also doubt that a vast majority of the fans turned against college basketball because of the scandal. I would say the only major factor which contributes to lack of spectator interest to ordinary scheduled games at the Garden is lack of competition."

It was true that some of the New York schools had deemphasized after the scandal and the competition was not as good as before. But the game grew and prospered in other sections of the country, and in these areas the formula was the same one Ned Irish used: doubleheaders. The Chicago Stadium featured Loyola, DePaul, Northwestern and other Big Ten teams.

In Philadelphia, the Big Five, St. Joseph's, Penn, Villanova, La Salle and Temple, still played doubleheaders, but on the Pennsylvania campus, not in Convention Hall. There were doubleheaders in the Carolinas —in Greensboro, Raleigh and Charlotte. St. Bonaventure, Canisius and Niagara were the featured teams in Buffalo.

On the outside, Ned Irish seemed to be a tough, hard businessman. His friends claim he was extremely shy, likable and misunderstood. He was also sentimental —and he did a great deal for basketball in this country.

"I get a lot of pleasure," he said, "from the feeling that I was part of the growth of the game from an insignificant sectional sport to one that draws more spectators every year than any other. It's a wonderfully exciting game, and the more attractive it is, the better I feel about it—no matter where it's played."

7

BOB PETTIT
Symbol of Class

It was early March, 1965 and Ben Kerner, a tough, unyielding businessman who owned the St. Louis Hawks, walked to a lectern, put some papers down, adjusted his glasses and began reading. Midway through the announcement, Kerner began to sob and choke on his words.

Mike Aubuchon, the attorney for the Hawks, moved to Kerner's side and guided him gently away from the lectern. Then Aubuchon finished the statement about the retirement of the man who had brought a new grace, a new look to professional basketball, a man who had been most responsible for making Ben Kerner's professional life successful.

That man was Bob Pititt, the lean, graceful forward of the St. Louis Hawks, the man with the feathery, soft jump shot, the first player in the history of the National Basketball Association to score 20,000 points.

"I could speak for hours on Bob's accomplishments and the contributions he has made to basketball," Kerner had said in his statement. "All these are engraved in the record books . . . There may have been greater players, but none with greater desire and dedication."

For Bob Pettit, basketball was a series of adjustments. And the adjusting for this intelligent young man began early, not far from the campus of Louisiana State University in Baton Rouge where later he would become an All-America selection.

At 14, Robert E. Lee Pettit, an only child, was 5-feet-10 inches and 118 pounds. He enjoyed all sports, but somehow was having a lot of trouble with all of them. "I went out for the freshman football team at Baton Rouge High," Pettit later recalled, "but my career lasted one play. The ball-carrier went through my position (right tackle) for 65 yards.

"In freshman basketball I got in for three games and didn't score a point. Then I went out for the freshman baseball team, and was the first boy cut from the squad. The next year the coach of the J.V. baseball team ran out of uniforms before he got to me. I hate to think what the effect of that brushoff would have been if my dad had not tempered it by putting up a basket in our back yard. Maybe I'm over-dramatizing the incident, but I believe it was the turning point of my life, and I don't mean just in basketball. My dad's understanding . . . helped me regain my confidence."

Bob remembers those days in the back yard vividly. "When it got dark," he said, "I'd put two chest-high lamps in the window facing the basket. That gave me enough light to practice some more." When the next season (Bob's sophomore year) rolled around, the skinny youngster decided to try for the high school team again. "All I was able to accomplish," he said, "was to immortalize my high school basketball coach, Kenner Day."

Pettit explained that 17 players tried out for the team and 12 were selected. Pettit was one of the unlucky five. "Today," Bob jokes, "when they introduce him [Day] at banquets or write about him in the paper, they say, 'here's the man who cut Bob Pettit from his team.'

"How can you describe the hurt you feel when you are 14 and not good enough to make the team?" Bob continued. "It is the end of the world. You feel like a failure. You think everywhere you go people are looking at you and pointing a finger and talking about you in whispers. . . . It hurts to be unwanted—even if it is only by the high school basketball coach. At first I just moped around the house. Then I started to go down to my church. A bunch of the guys got together and we formed a three-team church league. All the players in the league were like me, high school dropouts."

The basket in the back yard and the Church League gave young Pettit more practice time. Finally, by his junior year, he made the high school team. His play wasn't spectacular and there were almost no hints that by his senior year he would develop the way he did.

By then, Bob was 6-foot-7 and his high school team won the state championship. He had been one of the major reasons for that success even though he had the mumps and missed several games during the regular season.

Bob's position in high school was center and that's what he played when he enrolled at LSU. He had a fairly good hook shot and jump shot at the time and had begun to develop into the fine rebounder he would become in the pros. Between 1951 and 1954, Pettit scored 2,002 points, and he made All-America for the first time in his junior year when he averaged 21.2 points per game. The next year he repeated as an All-America with a 31.4 average.

The Baltimore Bullets had the first choice in the NBA draft of college seniors that year and Baltimore selected

Frank Selvy, the nation's leading scorer with a 41-point average at Furman. Kerner's Hawks, then playing in Milwaukee, had second choice and they selected Bob Pettit who was now 6-foot-9. Bob asked for $15,000 and received $11,000 to sign his first contract, and now another transition loomed—from pivot man to forward.

"I was always a pivot man in high school and college, so I had to learn to play all over again," Bob said. "Everybody knows the obvious difference in the two positions, that you have to play facing the basket after years of having your back to it. But there are many more differences. When I played center, the guard brought the ball to me, but as a forward I had to maneuver for position along with the guards. They might be trying to feed me the ball, but I also had to learn to set picks for them or find ways to spring them loose.

"A forward has to know how to drive for the basket, moving from maybe 15 feet away instead of the seven or eight that a center moves. I was accustomed to getting many of my baskets on tip-ins, but as a forward I found that more often I had to catch the rebound and shoot. The technique is quite different."

There were other problems, too. "You've got to be in a spot where you can shoot if you get the ball," Pettit explained. "A good defensive man will work you into a corner, where you are all tied up. The idea is to be in a position from which you can shoot or drive around your man, or maybe bounce a pass to the center."

Bob was always a superbly conditioned athlete. "I don't get out of shape," he said. "So the conditioning work isn't especially hard for me. I never have a weight or a wind problem. My only objective in the early part of the season is strengthening my legs. It usually is not until December that my legs are at their best. The legs are the key to my main skills, shooting and rebounding."

You could tell from the beginning that Bob Pettit wasn't going to be any ordinary professional. That first season (1954–55) he was named Rookie of the Year after averaging 20.4 points and 13.8 rebounds per game. For 10 straight years he would lead the Hawks in both scoring and rebounding.

And for 10 straight years, before injuries plagued him in his last season, Pettit finished among the NBA's top five in scoring and rebounding. In 1955–56, his second season, he won the Most Valuable Player award after leading the league in scoring with a 25.7 average and in rebounding with a 16.2 mark. He won the MVP award once more for the 1958–59 season when he again led the league in scoring with a 29.2 average. He finished second to Bill Russell of Boston in rebounding with a 16.4 average.

Bob finished his 11-year career with some astonishing figures. He scored 20,880 points a figure which still placed him fifth on the all-time scoring list at the beginning of the 1971–72 season seven years after his retirement. He also ranked as the game's third leading rebounder behind Russell and Wilt Chamberlain. His lifetime scoring average was 26.4 and his rebounding total was 12,851; he was named the MVP of the league All-Star game four times.

After the 1954–55 season, Kerner moved the Hawks' franchise to St. Louis where—thanks mostly to Pettit—the team thrived at the gate. Bob's improvement and the team's seemed to grow every year. By 1957–58, the Hawks were World Champions, defeating the Boston Celtics. In the deciding game, Pettit scored 50 points, including the final two points which gave the Hawks the title.

The next year was even better for Bob as an individual, but the Hawks didn't repeat as champions. In fact, their one victory marked the only time the Boston Celtics didn't win in a 10-year stretch.

But Bob's play continued to amaze everyone around the league. It wasn't just his scoring that impressed fans and players, but his rebounding, too. "I take a lot of pride in rebounding," he once explained. "It sets the tone for my entire game because it's largely a matter of desire. The first item I look at in the box score is the rebounds. Ask any big man."

Ed Macauley, Pettit's teammate and later his coach, never stopped talking about Bob's value to the Hawks. "He is a miracle of consistent class," Macauley said. "What you notice about him is that he's fast, he makes every move count, he's smart, he has a wonderful touch with the ball. . . . The reason for this is that Bob makes every inch and pound work for him as he does his job."

Bill Russell, who had many memorable duels with Pettit on the backboards, remembers that Bob "made 'second effort' a part of the sport's vocabulary. He kept coming at you more than any man in the game. He was always battling for position, fighting you off the boards."

And Kerner will never forget Pettit's contributions to St. Louis basketball for it was just a few seasons after Bob's retirement that the Hawks' attendance began to fall and Kerner sold the team to a group in Atlanta. "I can only say this about Bobby," Kerner said in 1964. "He has made a complete difference in my life. If it weren't for Pettit, I am sure I would have been out of the game, broke and disillusioned a long time ago.

"I had the feeling after meeting Bobby and watching him play a few games that if we could get a bit of a break some place, he could make the difference.

Actually, it wasn't that he was the first great player we had. We had quite a few good ones. Mel Hutchins is one who comes to mind. We had to sell him to Fort Wayne to keep going. But there was something about Pettit that produced an air of electricity at the games."

Maybe that "something" was his intense concentration which began long before game time. Before home games at Kiel Auditorium in St. Louis, Bob made a late afternoon pilgrimmage for a half-hour shooting practice. "This not only tones up my shooting but it gets my legs in shape," Pettit explained. "I'd like to do it on the road and occasionally I have the chance—but sometimes it's difficult to find somebody with a key or find any towels, or, for that matter, even a basketball."

"The business about shooting," Kerner said, "is only part of it. Bobby wants to get off by himself and gear himself mentally for the game. That's how dedicated he is."

Bob said he didn't understand what could be so unusual about that ritual and about his overall dedication. "What it is with me, I guess," he said, "is that you go along in life and work hard, you reach new plateaus of accomplishment. With each plateau you reach, the demands upon you become greater. And your pride increases to meet the demands. . . . You build an image of yourself that has nothing to do with ego—but it has to be satisfied. When I fall below what I know I can do, my belly growls and growls. Anytime I'm not playing up to my best I can count on a jolt of indigestion."

Perhaps the philosophy was a bit extreme, but it was Pettit's style, and he and his teammates—and Kerner —were the beneficiaries. "His greatest season—his greatest contribution—was in 1961–62 when a multitude of circumstances found us having a bad year,"

Kerner said. "He never stopped hustling, never faltered one iota when you might expect a player to take it easy since obviously the cause was a futile one. Yet, Bob came through with a magnificent year, battling as only he can, to give our club some semblance of respectability."

Quite simply, Pettit had an insatiable appetite for excellence which was reflected not only in statistics but also in the fact that he made the league's all-star squad (first team) for 10 straight years.

The promise of a fine start on a banking and business career helped shape Bob's mind about retirement, and he decided to play one last season— 1964–65. ". . . I explained that after I had passed the 20,000-point plateau, there would be nothing left for me in the game. I would have had all the personal and team honors I possibly could win. The funny thing is that I felt I could play perhaps two more years and still maintain an average of 20 points a game, but I didn't want to continue like that. I could feel the spring going from legs and realized everything from then on would be downhill and I wanted to retire on top," he said.

And that is what Bob Pettit did. Despite injuries that final season, he still averaged 22.5 points and 12 rebounds a game. So on a March day in Baltimore it ended and that magnificent jump shot, those clutch rebounds, those painstaking moments on the foul line became a memory for all who ever saw him—a very vivid one which wouldn't be diluted by time.

8

BOB KURLAND
Oklahoma Foothills

The names jump off the cracked, yellowing pages of the old newspapers, reviving memories of another one of the eras that played such a major role in the development of basketball: the Phillips Oilers . . . the Denver Truckers . . . the Oakland Bittners . . . the Akron Goodyear Wingfoots . . . the Peoria Caterpillar-Diesels. . . .

These are the most memorable names from amateur basketball, and when one talks of the amateur game in this country and the amateur league that flourished during the 1940s and 1950s, one name dwarfs all the others. It is that of Bob Kurland, the 7-foot center from the Phillips Oilers, who also were known as the 66ers.

Bob Kurland, three-time All-American for Henry Iba at Oklahoma A&M; Bob Kurland, two-time member of the United States Olympic team; Bob Kurland, the man who turned down all that cash to sit behind a desk in Bartlesville, Oklahoma.

Amateur basketball was as much a way of life to Midwesterners as the college game or the pro game was to the city dwellers in New York or Philadelphia. And in Bartlesville, home base of the Phillips Petroleum Company, sponsors of the 66ers, Bob Kurland was as big a hero as Joe Lapchick in New York, Adolph Rupp in Kentucky or George Mikan in Minneapolis.

Between 1943 and 1948, the 66ers won five national titles and members of the team represented the United States in the 1948 and 1952 Olympiads. Kurland was on both teams. He also played on three of the Phillips national champions and made the All-AAU team from 1946 through 1952.

Bob Kurland was born December 23, 1924, in St. Louis, Missouri. The Kurlands were not surprised when young Bob began growing out of his clothes at a rapid pace. His father was 6-3, his mother 5-9.

As a child, Bob was too big to compete with the children from the neighborhood. At the age of thirteen, he already was 6-6. So he spent a lot of time alone fishing along the banks of the Mississippi and hunting game in the countryside. Finally, at Jennings High School, he started playing basketball.

It was not easy. He was not a natural athlete. Sometimes his feet moved in one direction, his body in another, his head in a third direction. But his coach, Walter Hulon, thought the boy had talent and he wrote a letter to his college friend Henry Iba, who was coaching basketball at Oklahoma A&M, now Oklahoma State.

Iba worked with Kurland during the summer months, and he recalls a day when the youngster tried 600 hook shots with his left hand. The first 100 hit neither the rim nor the backboard. The next 100 hit the backboard but didn't go in. After that, he began to improve. It was hard to be much worse.

Kurland enrolled at Oklahoma State, where he was

tagged with the nickname "Foothills." At the time, freshmen were eligible for varsity play, so he played in 21 games during the 1942–43 season, scoring only 53 points as a substitute for an average of 2.5 points per game. During that year, however, Kurland developed the art of goaltending (batting the ball away from the basket) to such a degree that people began questioning the legality of his move.

The next season, Kurland was a starter and developed his talent even more. His scoring improved, too, and he wound up with 444 points and a 13.4 average. He made the All-American team for the first time that season. He also made an impression on the rulesmakers of college basketball.

They were upset with the way Kurland batted the ball away from the basket whenever he was in a position to do so, which was often. During the 1943–44 season, the National Collegiate Athletic Association dispatched one of its officials to a game between Oklahoma A&M and the University of Oklahoma.

"They built a platform over the goal at Oklahoma U.," Kurland said, "and an NCAA official sat up there to see if I was putting my hand over the hoop, which was illegal, or just batting the ball away before it got to the hoop. I'm sure the official sitting up there was more distracting to Oklahoma than I was."

By the next season, the rule had been changed. It was now illegal to hit the ball on the downward flight. The rule ended defensive goaltending but it didn't end Kurland's career as some predicted it would.

"It will make a better player of the long dog," Iba said good-naturedly. "Last year, Bob was chosen on the All-America team chiefly for his goaltending and the points he dunked through the hoop. When Kurland parked himself under the other team's basket, he couldn't grab rebounds off the backboard and he wasn't in position to get downcourt fast enough to participate in our offense when we got possession of the ball. The rule will make him a more valuable team man for 40 minutes."

The new rule did not embitter Kurland. "This," he said, "is how progress is made. There were lots of boys who could jump high enough and who had good enough timing even then to make the rule change necessary. I guess we were just the first to develop a real goaltending defense and I suppose, more or less, the rule was changed because of me."

Perhaps, then, the 1944–45 season was Bob Kurland's greatest as a collegian. The rule change had put him under intense pressure. Could he and Oklahoma A&M challenge for the national championship?

Not only did they challenge, but they won it, defeating New York University, 49–55, before a record 18,035 in Madison Square Garden. Kurland, who averaged a then amazing 17 points per game, scored 22 points in the title game.

That same season there was a showdown game between the winner of the National Invitation Tournament, DePaul, with George Mikan in the lineup, against Oklahoma A&M with Kurland. The game raised $50,000 for the American Red Cross. Oklahoma A&M won, 41–38, with Kurland scoring 14 points against 9 for Mikan.

Mikan fouled out, but Kurland had dominated the game until then. He was an awesome figure on defense and though he did not goaltend, De Paul, concerned with his presence, made only 16 of 96 shots. Asked about his frequent college battles with Mikan, Kurland replied, "He thought he did very well and I thought I did very well. Individually, I think he made more total points."

The following season, 1945–46, Oklahoma A&M

won its second straight national title. When the Cow-pokes beat North Carolina before 18,479 at Madison Square Garden, it marked the first time any team had won the championship twice in a row.

Kurland, the leading scorer in the nation that season (643 points, 19.4 average) scored 23 in the title game. He won the scoring title with a spectacular 307-point explosion in his last twelve games. Although he seldom went for the big score—he preferred, as did Iba, to concentrate on defense—he had a sensational night on February 22, 1946. That night, Ed Macauley of St. Louis University, considered one of the best defensive players in basketball, was guarding him, but Kurland didn't seem to mind. He scored 58 points and astounded the whole country with his performance.

When his collegiate career ended, Kurland was besieged with offers from the professionals. One team offered $60,000 for five years. Another club offered $30,000 for two years. But Kurland decided not to play professional basketball. He joined Phillips Petroleum. "When I got out of college," he said, "pro basketball wasn't nearly as attractive as it is now."

Kurland was a good catch for the company. In addition to being a fine basketball player, he was an outstanding young executive with a warm personality. At the time, Phillips already had the best team in amateur basketball, and when Kurland joined them, they became even better. For six years he led the 66ers in scoring and set a record of 787 points in a season and had a career record of 4,092 points.

The 66ers played a long schedule, sometimes as many as sixty or more games during a season. Kurland's most memorable performance for Phillips came in 1948, when the University of Kentucky, the national collegiate champions, and the 66ers, met in Madison

Square Garden for the championship of the Olympic trials.

At halftime the score was tied. Then in the second half, Kurland hooked in three quick baskets to give the 66ers a comfortable lead, which they maintained and parlayed into a final 53–49 victory. Kurland, meanwhile, held Kentucky's All-American, Alex Groza, to one field goal and two free throws, while scoring 20 points himself. Basketball writers claim it was one of the best games ever played.

At the Olympic Games in Harrington Arena, London, Groza and Kurland gave the United States an unbeatable combination. Only 82 persons were present for the opening program, but it didn't bother the American team. They swept through their eight games, crushing France, 65–21, in the final. Groza led the American scorers at the Games with 76 points, followed by Kurland with 65.

In 1952 at Helsinki, Finland, Bob teamed with Clyde Lovellette, the 6-8 Kansas star, to give the U.S. another strong combination up front. The U.S. had won 7 games to reach the finals against Russia, a team it had defeated, 86–58, earlier.

This time the Russians decided to hold the ball in the title game. After 10 minutes the score was 4–3, U.S. leading. The Americans eventually won, 36–25, with Lovellette and Kurland the "leading scorers" with 9 and 8 points, respectively.

The red-headed Kurland decided to quite basketball after his appearance in the 1952 Olympic Games. "Each season the game seems to get a little harder to play," he said. "The schedule is a little longer and finally it ceases to be enjoyment. In my opinion, that's the time to quit. That time for me has arrived."

Meanwhile, AAU basketball continued, but it seemed to lack something after Kurland's retirement and gradually declined until the final blow in April of 1968, when Phillips announced it would no longer sponsor a team.

And with that announcement came an end to basketball history. No longer would there be a hushed silence in the Bartlesville Field House as Frank Phillips and his wife, Jane, took their seats before a 66ers basketball game.

And no longer would many of the radio sets in the state be tuned for the nightly games during AAU tournament week in Denver. Amateur basketball had done much for the game and Bob Kurland had done much for amateur basketball.

A few years after his retirement, Kurland looked back at the game and the changes that he forced and the changes that came later. "The greatest change," he said, "is in the minds of the coaches. The coach now is aware of the fact that a man over 6-6 potentially can perform as well as his smaller counterpart.

"The early training of the big boys is now geared to developing a player who can perform in all phases of the game rather than that of only a rebounder, a post man and a passer. As a result, today we have boys playing who are schooled in what was once the little man's game.

"It is an ancient adage that a good big man can beat a good little man. For many years no one in basketball believed this. It took the example of a few exceptional boys to prove this point.

"As a defensive measure other coaches were forced to find big men and work with them to develop their skills and ability so that they could offset a few exceptions. The boys with size and talent were always there but the coaches did not want to exert the effort, nor did they know how to develop the boys.

"As the picture became clear, it showed plainly that

the better teams had the big man. The game today has evolved into a big man's game with the exception being the little man performing on the same floor. Bob Cousy was an example of this.

"The stars are men like Chamberlain and Russell, who, had they played fifteen years before, would have been outstanding but not to the degree that they are today because of the fact that the game was not geared to their potential, nor would most of the coaches of that time have realized the possibilities they had in their hands.

"The game now is better not because of rule changes, a better ball and bigger crowds, but because coaching has finally caught up and they are working to get the maximum out of the material available."

And today, Bob Kurland is one of the most respected executives with the Phillips Petroleum Co. He put business and basketball together and came out ahead in both professions.

9

FORREST "PHOG" ALLEN
Dr. Foghorn

On legal documents it was Dr. Forrest C. Allen. The formality ended there. To everyone in basketball the name was Phog Allen, the nickname a derivative of the term "foghorn."

There are a few nicknames in sport more fitting than Allen's. He got it while umpiring baseball games in the early 1900s. They called him "Foghorn" then, but one day a sportswriter decided to get fancy and wrote it "Phog," and it stuck.

Though Allen never pursued his career as a baseball umpire, he always managed to get the maximum from his well-exercised vocal cords. Was he simply a windbag, or was he, as some suggest, a prophet? Outspoken and colorful, he never missed the chance to take a verbal slap at those he felt were in need of a lecture.

He also earned the title of "Dr.," which preceded his name. His degree was from the Kansas City School of Osteopathy, the year 1912. He never devoted full time to a practice, but he did treat many people, including many of the big names in sport. He cured baseball star Johnny Mize of an arm ailment and also treated football immortal George Halas. He never lost his interest in the study of athletic injuries, and always was in the forefront when it came to research and new discoveries in that field.

Whatever the subject, basketball or medicine, Phog was an expert. His opinions were strong and very often unpopular. In the end, however, he was often more right than wrong.

Take his statement in 1944 when he predicted a major-college basketball scandal. Everybody laughed at the idea. "The Foghorn is sounding again," one paper proclaimed. Ned Irish of Madison Square Garden was infuriated by Allen's comments which pinpointed the Garden as the center of collegiate-basketball gambling.

One scandal erupted in 1945, then in 1951 a larger one almost ruined the game. Nobody was laughing at Allen then. His station as one of the most successful basketball coaches of all time gave him a platform and outlet for his opinions.

Phog Allen and the game started at almost the same time. He grew up in Independence, Missouri, and lived on the same block with President-to-be Harry S. Truman. The youngster seemed intrigued by basketball, and in 1904 he joined the Kansas City Athletic Club team and became one of its stars. The other player of distinction was Jesse James, Jr., whose father also had an accurate shot.

At the time, the Buffalo Germans had the best basketball team in the country and were considered national champions. Allen decided his team could beat Buffalo, so he raised $500 as a guarantee to the Germans and they came to Kansas City for a three-game series. Buffalo won the first game but Kansas City took the next two, 30–28 and 45–15, and Allen became a hero in the Midwest.

At the University of Kansas, Allen was an outstanding player. He set a single-game scoring record of 26 points which stood until 1939. His coach at Kansas was Dr. James Naismith, the inventor of the game. The two became great friends even though their outlooks differed on some subjects. Coaching was one.

During the 1908–09 season Allen did something no other coach has ever duplicated. He simultaneously coached three different teams to a combined 74–10 record. Kansas had a 25–3 mark; Baker University a 22–2 record; and the Haskell Indian School was 27–5.

The students at Baker University had written a letter to Naismith asking if it would be possible for Allen to coach their team while he was coaching at Kansas.

Naismith, a smile on his face, then went to Allen to discuss the subject. "I've got a good joke on you," he said. "They want you to coach basketball at Baker."

"What's funny about that?" Allen replied.

"Heavens, man," Naismith said. "You don't coach basketball. You just play it."

"Why can't *you* coach it?" Allen countered. "You do other games."

Naismith shook his head and laughed heartily. Many years later, though, the game's father would inscribe a picture for Allen. It read: "From the Father of Basketball to the Father of Basketball Coaches."

From 1909 through 1912, Allen studied osteopathy, and didn't return to basketball until the 1912–13 season with the Warrensburg (Missouri) Teachers. His reasons for studying medicine were quite simple. "After I started coaching," he said, "I felt that I should learn more about a boy's body structure instead of simply what made him a good basketball player."

Allen's insights into the medical world helped in the formation of his philosophies concerning basketball coaching. His approach to the game was a very simple one: natural body movements must be utilized by the coaches and athletes.

It sounded strange, even comical, listening to Allen explain his "ape man" theory which put every player into a crouch whether he was playing offense or defence. "Look at any animal," Allen explained. "Whether attacking or defending, he assumes a semi-crouching position. How can you react otherwise? The knees are the only springs in the body. Bend them slightly and you can make any move rapidly required in basketball."

A famous short movie titled "Killing the Killer" became a standard part of Allen's teaching. The movie showed a fight to the death between a mongoose and a cobra. Allen would show the movie once a year to his players, pointing out that the mongoose won what seemed to be an uneven match because it had "deft movements."

"We tell our boys who are learning individual defense to imagine that their arms are cut off at their elbows," Allen said. "When they do this they realize that their feet are their biggest weapons. They'll shift to meet every situation and always be in position. There is far too much use of arms and far too little of feet in basketball.

"In the ape stance on defense I have my boys yell," he continued. "We don't yell all the time—only when it's appropriate. My boys have their arms raised and their hands like a claw in the opponent's face. Man has been clutching at one another's throat for 100,000 years, and when my boys are in that stance and yell, sometimes the ball is dropped and rolls into our hands."

His animal-anatomy analogies didn't end there. "Lucky," he often said, "is the young boy who has a frisky dog with which to play. Watch the boy trying to pin down the dog as he crouches, feints and dodges. Pretty soon the boy is crouching, too. He is shifting his feet. He does not become overbalanced reaching in any direction. This is informal play, but the boy is learning to apply fundamentals that will carry him in basketball."

Playing basketball for Kansas became a unique experience. In modern terms it also was something of a "happening." There were few dull moments.

Allen spent seven years at Warrensburg, where he compiled a 107–7 record. Then he returned to Kansas, where he remained until he was forced into retirement at the age of seventy following the 1955–56 season. During the years at Kansas his teams won 591 games and lost 219, with the 1922–23, 1923–24 and 1951–52 teams winning national championships.

In forty-eight years of coaching, Allen's teams won 771 games while losing only 233. His Kansas clubs won or shared thirty championships as members of the Missouri Valley, Big Six and Big Seven conferences.

Several of the country's greatest coaches learned the game from Allen during that time, including Arthur "Dutch" Lonborg, John Bunn, Adolph Rupp, Forrest Cox and Louis Menze. Lonborg earned his fame at Northwestern, Bunn at Stanford, Rupp at Kentucky, Cox at Colorado and Menze at Iowa State.

Allen was an outstanding coach, and his individualism made him an unforgettable man. There was no institution sacred to Phog Allen. He always managed to embroil himself in some type of controversy, whether it concerned rules, personalities or the Eastern basketball establishment.

He was one of the first coaches to plead for the raising of the baskets from 10 to 12 feet so the game would not be dominated by the "goons." Allen then gave his critics all the ammunition they needed for an assault on him when he signed two of the greatest "goons" in the history of the game for Kansas, Clyde Lovellette and Wilt Chamberlain.

One of Allen's pet projects concerned a commissioner for college athletics. Allen proposed that the czar draw a salary of $100,000 and rule the college scene with a strong arm. This way, he said, college sports would be free of undesirable people and ideas. Allen had the perfect man for the job: himself.

Allen won his share of the headlines with that proposal and many others. He had no fears about tackling any issue regarding collegiate athletics.

In 1935 he charged that college athletes were persecuted because of academic standards that were too strict. In 1942 he said college stars were evading income taxes and charged that some made between $10,000 and $20,000 a year. And in 1945 he accused gamblers of knowing more about big-time football teams than the coaches and athletic directors.

Criticism never seemed to bother him—and he was the object of a great deal of it, especially during the period when Lovellette was the prime high school prospect in the country.

Lovellette was a high school star in Terre Haute, Indiana, and when he finally decided to enroll at Kansas, Allen calmly announced that Clyde selected the school because the air on Mt. Oread, where the campus was located, was good for his asthma.

Big Clyde hardly played like an asthmatic. He was a 6-9, 244-pounder with blond hair and a huge lantern jaw who answered to the nickname of the "big white whale." During the 1951–52 season the Jayhawks won 28 of 31 games and lost to the Peoria Caterpillar-Diesels by 2 points in the finals of the Olympic basketball trials. The Jayhawks had won the National Collegiate championship a few weeks earlier.

Despite the loss in the trials, Kansas players formed the backbone of the U.S. team. Seven of Allen's players made the trip to Helsinki, Finland. At the 1952 Olympics, Lovellette teamed with 7-foot Bob Kurland of the Phillips Oilers to give the United States an unbeatable front-court punch.

It was particularly gratifying for Allen to see the United States win the gold medal that year, for he had led the fight, beginning as far back as 1927, to have basketball included in the Olympic program.

Allen was extremely active in the administrative side of basketball throughout his career. He was one of the founders and the first president of the National Basketball Coaches Association. He also helped start the national college championship tournament, and no major rules change was considered without first consulting him. He campaigned successfully for the 10-second rule to speed up the game, but he was unsuccessful in having the center jump reinstated after its elimination in 1937. Fan-shaped backboards were his innovation, and he tried to start a movement against the bonusfoul rule. "Only alcoholics," he said, "want two shots for one."

It was a typical Allen comment. He was a witty, intelligent man who never lacked for ideas. Some were good, some bad, but all were interesting and provocative. For example, the stories about his pregame routine are legend. When his team played at home, Phog met the players at 3:30 P.M. and took them to a large dormitory filled with beds for everyone, including the coach. A nap of an hour or more was mandatory.

After awakening, Allen took the players on a mile walk, then at five-thirty they sat down to a dinner that consisted of two slices of wholewheat toast, a portion of honey, a half grapefruit and celery. Sometimes he added a cup of hot chocolate to the menu.

Allen had a phobia about cold feet, so he next led the team into a room where there was a large fireplace. The players had to place their bare feet close to the fire. Allen, of course, had a very simple explanation: "I never saw a man with cold feet who wasn't nervous and jumpy. Keep the feet warm and you keep the nerves of the players calm."

Someone once remarked of Phog Allen that "he has done everything in basketball but put the bounce in the ball."

"Yeah," remarked a listener, "but he has enough wind to do that, too."

More often than not the windstorms he created had a cleansing effect, stripping away much extraneous matter and exposing only the essentials of a problem or idea.

A lot of people laughed at him, a lot were angry with him and a lot could not tolerate his pointed barbs. Behind all the talk, though, there was a man who knew the game of basketball and could teach it.

There were few better teachers. In fact, the only better one in terms of won-lost record was Adolph Rupp. And where did Adolph Rupp learn the game? From Phog Allen at the University of Kansas.

10

ED MACAULEY
"Easy" is the Name

Ed Macauley, who was best known by his nickname, "Easy Ed," did more than simply awaken a city and convert it into a basketball town. He also proved that the big man, like the clever guards and smooth forwards, could bring grace and deftness to basketball.

Macauley helped change a lot of things in basketball, the most important being the image of the big man, who, until Ed began playing the game, had been classified as a "goon." The big men in the pre-Macauley era simply overpowered opponents because of their bulk and size and little else.

That wasn't Macauley's style. "Easy Ed" was a slender, stoop-shouldered young man who stood 6-8 and weighed between 180 and 190 pounds. He gained his fame as an All-American at St. Louis University and later professionally with the Boston Celtics and the St. Louis Hawks.

It was during his college career that he made his biggest impression on the game and the public. "They don't call him 'Easy Ed' for nothing," said Macauley's coach at St. Louis University, Ed Hickey. "His unusual muscular coordination and rhythm more than make up for his lack of heft. I have never seen a smoother player. He handles a basektball as gracefully as Fritz Kreisler does a violin."

Macauley played the middle for the Billikens, making the All-American team as a junior during the 1947–48 season, when St. Louis won the National Invitation Tournament title at Madison Square Garden. He also made All-American the following year.

There were times when Macauley was faced with frightening matchups in the pivot. Players 40 and 50 pounds heavier, and some even an inch or two taller, would be assigned to guard him. When the scoreboard clock showed 00:00, usually the bigger men either were on the bench with five personal fouls or their faces were a mirror of the frustration they felt in trying to outduel Macauley.

"Easy Ed" never wasted a moment or a move on the basketball court. He was one of those people blessed with a hidden sense, which made him master of his profession. Bob Considine, the syndicated columnist, watched Macauley play and wrote:

> He's the best player I've seen since Hank Luisetti. He's one of the few giants who is not a freak or goon. He moves with the grace and ease of a good lightweight, scorning the senseless pell-melling around the court, always knows what he's doing, and is as proficient on defense as he is when he's dunking the ball through the basket.

Macauley's delicate, pale features and his narrow waist and slender body made him seem as fragile as a piece of Limoges china. A healthy shock of brown hair gave him a Li'l Abner look. Females in the crowds at the St. Louis U. games immediately wanted to mother him. The men winced or looked the other way when he tried to maneuver through the defensive triangle for a rebound, which he had no business grabbing but often did.

Macauley was born in St. Louis on March 22, 1928. The fact that he was a native son made him one of the most popular athletic figures in St. Louis history.

When he was two weeks old, there came a hint of what was in his future—he had outgrown his bassinet. By the time he was fourteen, he was 6-6, but he was not a natural athlete. He had to work at basketball.

When he was a freshman at St. Louis University High School, he could not try out for the basketball team, because a late class conflicted with the team's scheduled practice sessions. Each day, after the team had finished practicing, young Ed would show up, ask the custodian for a basketball and shoot baskets until it was time to close the gymnasium.

He had no schedule conflicts the following year and made the team. In his final two seasons he led the club in scoring, attracting a number of scouts from the major college teams.

But there was no doubt where he would go: St. Louis University. He had developed a strong allegiance to the area and wanted to remain close to home, where his father, a prominent attorney, had been confined to the house following an automobile accident.

St. Louis never had been a basketball town. Baseball was the sport with the Cardinals and Browns monopolizing most of the sports news. In the winter, crowds of 300 or 400 were normal for St. Louis University basketball games. Even the St. Louis Bombers, a professional team, had difficulty drawing.

Then Ed Macauley changed everything. He was, as they say in show business, box office. Before he wore the St. Louis University uniform, the school played its games in a small campus gymnasium. But when the team started to win and Macauley began to stir the fans, the team moved to the 11,000-seat Municipal Auditorium downtown.

The big seasons came in 1947–48 and 1948–49, when Ed was named to the All-American teams. In 1947–48, St. Louis University finished with a 22–3 record and then tacked on 3 more victories to win the NIT.

Ed averaged a modest 13.5, but he had an excellent year defensively, continually stopping the opposition's offensive stalwarts. In the NIT title game, for example, Macauley was matched against Dolph Schayes of NYU, who later became one of the great professionals.

Hickey, knowing Macauley's deep feelings for his team, took the youngster aside. "Ed," he said, "the team still comes first, and I want you to keep playing the game the way you learned it. But don't be afraid to shoot."

Macauley wasn't. He scored 24 points as St. Louis won, 62–52, and he did such a strong defensive job on Schayes that Dolph's contribution to the NYU attack had been neutralized. Macauley won the Most Valuable Player award for his performance.

It was a national championship as far as St. Louis was concerned, with Macauley the toast of the nation. How did Macauley and his teammates celebrate their victory in the country's largest city? They went bowling and later they stopped at a bakery, bought a huge bag of pastries, had an urn of coffee sent to their hotel room and toasted their triumph.

Macauley always had deep respect for institutions and rules, but he also was a youngster with a deep-rooted sense of humor. Because of his height he had a lot of trouble finding beds large enough to provide him with a good night's sleep. In those days, St. Louis, like many other sports teams, traveled by train.

Macauley had to occupy two upper berths on those trips. At the time the athletic director at St. Louis was a man named Bill Durney, and on trips, shortly before the team retired for the night, he would tour the aisles, checking to see if everything was all right with the players.

One night Macauley spotted Durney and said in a concerned voice, "I'm worried, Bill."

"Why, whatsamatter?" Durney replied, alarmed that something was bothering the team's star player. "Are you sick?"

"No," Macauley answered, "but I understand somebody left a morning call for seven-fifteen for that berth and for seven-thirty for this one. You know what that'll mean?"

"No, what?" Durney said.

"That'll mean," Macauley said, a grin splitting his face, "that they'll wake up my feet before my head."

Luckily Macauley got his rest and St. Louis its victories. During Macauley's junior year, the team finished 25–3 and the following year, when it won the Sugar Bowl tournament, it was 22–4. St. Louis University was now famous. So was the coach—and, of course, so was Macauley, whose picture was being carried coast to coast by the wire services and the news magazines.

Hickey had a deep admiration for Macauley. "He's a great trouper," the coach said. "He's much like the plot of a mystery novel. He doesn't begin to unfold until late in the book."

The professionals were also impressed by Macauley, and one scout predicted that he would be a 30-point-per-game man when he joined the professional league.

Dr. James Naismith coaches his son, Jim, in 1925.   UPI.

George Mikan, DePaul University '46.

Nat Holman was the Original Celtics' clean-cut hero.
Joe Lapchick Collection.

Left. "Easy" Ed Macauley and his Celtic teammate, Bob Cousy. UPI.

Right. Angelo (Hank) Luisetti, Stanford University '38.

Bob Kurland — seven feet of talent.

Ned Irish as president of the N.Y. Knicks.

Madison Square Garden.

Bob Pettit is on the dribble against Lakers' Tom Hawkins.

UPI.

Some of Kate Smith's Celtics: (from left) Nat Hickey, Dutch Dehnert, Joe Lapchick, Miss Smith, Pat Herlihy, Ed Burke, Davey Banks.

Dutch Dehnert Collection.

The Renaissance, one of the great basketball teams of all time. Left to right: Clarence "Fat" Jenkins, Bill Yancey, John Holt, James "Pappy" Ricks, Eyre Saitch, Charles "Tarzan" Cooper and "Wee Willie" Smith. Inset: Owner Robert L. Douglas who organized club in 1922-23.

The Man and the Master: UCLA head basketball coach John Wooden (right) delivering a few words of cage wisdom to Bruin Center Lew Alcindor, now Kareem Abdul-Jabbar and star in pro basketball.

UCLA.

Dolph Schayes of the Syracuse Nationals.

As a pro with the Chicago Stags, Phillip (19) attempts to block a shot by New York's Paul Noel. UPI.

Top left. Dr. Forrest "Phog" Allen.

Top right. Henry (Hank) Iba: elected as coach—1968.

Left. Clair Francis Bee: elected as coach–1967.

Below left. Arnold J. "Red" Auerbach: elected as coach—1968.

Below right. Adolph F. Rupp: elected as coach—1968.

His family, however, wanted him to pass up professional ball in favor of a law career. Macauley had to gently tell his parents no. The Bombers, the hometown team, were struggling, but they had one hope—to have Macauley in uniform for the 1949–50 season.

Even Macauley's presence wasn't enough to save the club, which folded at the end of the year. Ned Irish wanted Macauley for his New York franchise, so he tried to buy the entire Bomber franchise just to get Ed, who had become a favorite with the Madison Square Garden fans during the NIT. The league, for once, stood up to Irish, and Macauley wound up with the Boston Celtics.

At Boston he teamed with Bob Cousy and Bill Sharman to make basketball nearly as popular there as hockey and baseball. Until then it had struggled for acceptance. So now Macauley could claim that he had much to do with the success of the sport in two of the nation's biggest cities.

The fans loved the Celtics and the smooth ball-handling of Cousy and Macauley and the great shooting of Sharman. Macauley never was strong enough to become one of the pro greats, but he did average 17.5 points per game (11,234 points) during a ten-year career with the Celtics and St. Louis Hawks. His defensive ability, combined with his offensive prowess, made him an exceedingly valuable player, a fact that both players and coaches realized. Their admiration earned him a spot on the NBA All-Star team seven times.

In 1956, Macauley figured in one of the most important transactions in the game's history. That year Ben Kerner, who owned the Hawks, had the draft rights to Bill Russell, the All-American center from the University of San Francisco.

Kerner wasn't sure that Russell planned to play in

the NBA. There were rumors that the 6-10 defensive ace would go to the Harlem Globetrotters instead. A practical man, Kerner decided not to gamble on Russell. He traded the draft rights to Boston for Macauley and Cliff Hagan.

It was a good trade—for the moment. Macauley and Hagan joined Bob Pettit in the St. Louis lineup and the Hawks made it to the championship playoffs in 1956–57, losing to the Celtics, who had signed Russell, 125–123, in the seventh game. The following season the Hawks reversed the outcome, defeating Boston in a six-game championship final.

It seemed a good time for Macauley to retire as an active player, and he did so with regret. But he was not out of professional basketball. Kerner, who hired and fired coaches as casually as he sat down to break-fast, thought it would be a good idea to hire Macauley when the Hawks started poorly during the 1958–59 season. The transition from player to coach wasn't difficult for Macauley. He coached the Hawks to a first-place finish after a 43–19 spree.

The Hawks were upset in the playoffs by the Minneapolis Lakers. There would be no championship that season. The following year, Macauley again guided the team to a first-place finish in the Western Division, and this time the Hawks made it to the NBA finals, only to lose to Boston again, 4 games to 3.

Two years was a relatively long time for a coach to work for Kerner. So Macauley, hoping to avoid the em-barrassment of another Kerner tirade, resigned and moved "upstairs" to the general manager's office. Op-portunities in television and radio beckoned, so Ed spent very little time as Hawk general manager, retiring before the 1960–61 season began. Thus ended the ca-reer of a very popular native son.

He had done much for basketball in his home town,

kindling spectator interest in the game when he was a collegian and then helping the Hawks sell professional ball in the area. He was, simply, the Renaissance man of St. Louis basketball.

11

JOE LAPCHICK
A Man for All Eras

Joe Lapchick's mother had washed his basketball uniform and had placed it on the line to dry. His father, a policeman in their home town of Yonkers, N.Y., came home later in the day and spotted the shirt and short pants.

"What is that?" he asked his son while pointing to the uniform.

"My basketball suit," young Lapchick replied.

"You mean," his father said, "you go out in front of people dressed like that?"

The year was 1912 and basketball was still in its infancy. Not many people, including Joe's father, knew much about the game.

But Joe, who was 6-3 when he was twelve, knew about the game and the game knew about him. He was considered a "giant," and therefore was a strong asset to any team.

Ironically, a church team called the Trinity Midgets was the first organized basketball squad that benefited from Joe Lapchick's presence. After the Trinity Midgets, there were many teams whose names would sound odd to modern fans but rekindle fond memories of the game's early history in older fans. Teams with names like the Hollywood Inn of Yonkers, the Whirlwinds and the Visitations of New York and the Bantams of Yonkers. Pay per game varied from $5 with the Bantams to $7 with the Whirlwinds. "You never knew who you were playing in those days," Lapchick said. "I was playing in four different leagues against the same group of fellows.

"They'd congregate at the information booth in Grand Central Station on the way to the games. You'd see a fellow and say, 'Who you playing with tonight?' He'd say, 'You.'

"They never talked about winning or losing, just about how they did against the men they covered. That was the standard of success. If you were the visiting club, it was pretty much taken for granted that you lost the game."

That is how it was in the early days of professional basketball, and Joe Lapchick was a professional from the earliest of those days. He drew his first paycheck from the Bantams in 1915 at the age of fifteen. It was for $5.

What made Joe Lapchick such an intriguing man was the fact that he and basketball literally grew up together. He was one of the few men who could truly claim that he had been part of every major era in basketball history, both ancient and modern, professional and collegiate.

There was something else that made Joe Lapchick unique. His whole life was dedicated to and bound up with the game of basketball. He was a wonderfully warm, pleasant man with the gift of making anyone feel at ease, whether that person was an old-timer in the game or a young reporter just starting on the basketball beat. It was not difficult for him to hold an audience for hours. His stories were rich and human, happy and sad, long and short. The history of the game had been filed neatly in his head.

For Lapchick, basketball had become profitable and a way of life by 1919, when he was making $10 a game, playing five and six nights a week. Soon he learned the fine art of playing one owner against the other and sometimes walking off with $75 a game. All the owners wanted him on their teams because by now he had grown to 6-5 and was the best center in the game.

"I was of the immigrant generation," Lapchick said, explaining why he started playing professional basketball so early. "Everybody had big families. We went right from grammar school to the factories. I thought anybody who went to high school was an intellectual. In those days, maybe 1 percent of those who played pro basketball had gone to college."

For Lapchick, "college" was his career with the Original Celtics, the finest basketball team in the world during the 1920s and 1930s. It was only natural that the Celtics would eventually sign Lapchick, the game's premier center. He joined the team at the end of the 1922–23 season, replacing the fabled Horse Haggerty.

It was the start of one of the great dynasties in sport. The Celtics, whose home base was New York, averaged 125 or 130 games a year, both in league and exhibition play. The team seldom lost more than 10 games in one season.

Lapchick always spoke lovingly of his days with the Celtics. "The team," he said, "had no time for alibis, excuses or explanations. The big asset was guts, and the only objective was to win basketball games.

"They were rough days and rough going. You carried your own uniform (always in need of laundering) from game to game, night after night, with or without sleep and with no relief for aches and pains.

"There was no training season. You got in shape by playing. If you complained about anything, you were gutless. One thing you quickly learned—to keep your fingernails trimmed and check your opponent's hands to make sure his nails were cut.

"The offense was a 'situation offense' much the same as I used with the Knickerbockers and at St. John's University. It was a freewheeling, fast-passing pressure offense by the greatest ballhandling team I ever saw. But there was no showboating. Every pass and every move had a purpose, and the technique broke the backs of practically every team we met.

"Defensively, you played your own man and no one else. He was your responsibility—you took care of him or else. There was no 'float' or 'sag.' You were completely on your own.

"I believe the Celtics were twenty years ahead of their time. They introduced switching on defense, give-and-go and pivot play; they were the first to operate as a unit with none of the members playing for other teams; they were the first to make use of peripheral vision. They never let the ball go carelessly and their shooting percentage was between .600 and .700. The Celtics took only perfect shots."

In addition to Lapchick, the Celtics had Nat Holman, who was the team's best scorer; Dutch Dehnert, the fine pivot player who complemented Lapchick so well in the lineup; Pete Barry, a "bear" off the boards; Johnny Beckman, the fiery leader and scorer; Nat Hickey, a good scorer and driver; and Davey Banks, the little man with the deadly set shot.

The Celtics played in the American Basketball League at the time, but by 1927 they were so good and had dominated it so completely that the league decided it would be in its best interests to break up the team. Lapchick, Dehnert and Barry wound up with Cleveland, Holman and Banks went to the New York Hakoahs and Beckman became manager of Baltimore.

The Cleveland Rosenblums, with the ex-Celtics as leaders, won two world's championships. But the team folded in the third year. Soon after, the league folded, too, and the Celtics regrouped and began barnstorming around the country in an old Pierce Arrow that cost $125.

Wherever the Celtics played they drew huge crowds. They continued to win through the early 1930s, but by the middle of the decade age began to tell and the team slowed down considerably. Soon players were retiring to enter coaching or other fields.

Lapchick went into coaching. The season was 1936–37, the school St. John's University in New York. Lapchick said he wouldn't have considered college coaching had it not been for Ned Irish, who began pushing the college game with his doubleheaders in Madison Square Garden.

Lapchick was not very sure of himself when he embarked on his coaching career. "During my entire career as a player," he said, "I never had the opportunity to come under the influence of a coach, as such. In fact, there were no coaches in professional basketball when I played. You learned basketball from experience and by watching, imitating and listening to the great players of the time. It was a system of trial and error with the emphasis on not making the same mistake twice.

"When I got to St. John's, I didn't know what to do. We never had a drill with the pros. All I knew was scrimmage and shoot."

Lapchick sought advice from his old teammates and from one of the men who would become one of his great coaching rivals, Clair Bee. "You know, Joe," Bee told him. "I used to go to Cleveland to see you guys play. I'd be ashamed to tell you anything."

Lapchick remembered the rest of the conversation. It made a deep impression. "Do the players call you Joe?" Bee asked. "Yes," Lapchick replied.

"That's a mistake," Bee said. "Make them call you coach or Mr. Lapchick."

"It was the finest advice I got," said Lapchick, who became one of the most successful of all college coaches. His career at St. John's was split into two parts by a stint as coach of the New York Knickerbockers.

His first stay at St. John's lasted from the 1936–37 season through 1947–48. He returned to St. John's for the 1956–57 campaign and remained with the Redmen until he retired at the end of the 1964–65 season.

His St. John's teams won 335 games and lost only 129. Among the 335 victories were four National Invitation Tournament championships. The first two were back-to-back: at the end of the 1942–43 season the Redmen defeated Toledo, 48–27; the next year they defeated DePaul and George Mikan, 47–39.

The DePaul game not only is memorable for what St. John's did on the basketball court but for what happened to Lapchick on the sidelines. An intense, gaunt man, Lapchick had difficulty controlling his emotions on the bench. To him a basketball game was agony. His wife seldom accompanied him to the games, because she couldn't bear to watch him go through the torture on the sidelines. He outdid himself in the NIT final against DePaul. But through this macabre experience, Joe Lapchick proved that his sense of humor was genuine.

The pressure on Lapchick and St. John's was tremendous. George Mikan, after all, was the premier player in college basketball, the game's greatest scorer at the time. With 10 minutes remaining, St. John's trailed by 3 points.

Lapchick stood up to make a substitution. A second later he was stretched out on the floor, unconscious. He regained consciousness a few minutes later, but by this time the Redmen had taken the lead. "I dealt strategy one helluva blow," Lapchick said. "I don't remember what substitution I wanted to make. It probably would have been wrong."

His fainting spell was only one of many other physical problems. He often complained of severe abdominal pains and he lost between 15 and 20 pounds during a season, making his thin frame seem ghostly on occasion.

Nevertheless, he decided to try professional coaching despite the rigors of the long, drawn-out schedule and the added number of games. He coached the Knickerbockers for nine seasons and three times his teams made it to the final round of the NBA playoffs. Twice the Knicks lost in the final minute of play in the title game.

The tension of pro ball forced Lapchick into the hospital several times. The doctors told him his problem was a simple one: nerves. "The trouble with you," one doctor told him, "is that day after day you're suffering what the average person suffers once or twice in a lifetime."

It was partially because of his health and partially because of a falling out with the Knicks' front office that Lapchick decided to retire from professional basketball and return to St. John's. "With the Knicks," he said, "I had lost the reins. If you don't hold the reins you're not a coach, no matter what else, no matter what technical basketball you teach."

Lapchick returned to St. John's when the school had

lost half of its 64 games. Lapchick quickly rebuilt the program and restored the school's prestige. During the 1958–59 season the Redmen won the Holiday Festival in Madison Square Garden, and in the finals of the NIT defeated Bradley in overtime, 76–71. Joe Lapchick was back.

He was an extremely popular man and as he approached his final year of coaching the sentiment grew. Nearly everywhere St. John's appeared that final year, the host schools made sure Lapchick was honored in a special ceremony before the game or at halftime.

Earlier that season his team had again won the Holiday Festival, upsetting the highly favored team from the University of Michigan, which featured Cazzie Russell, Bill Buntin and Oliver Darden.

St. John's did not have a powerful team. It was more of a hustling, scrappy team, one that had to scratch and claw for its victories. Little did Lapchick realize that it would give him the best of all possible send-offs.

Nobody expected the Redmen to be in the NIT finals that year, but on March 21, 1965, that's exactly where they were, opposite the tough Philadelphia team, Villanova.

The Garden was packed for Lapchick's farewell. Could the Redmen win it for him? Villanova was a slight favorite. Lapchick remembered back to the preseason predictions. "Everyone said we were just another team," he said.

The NIT committee had seeded the Redmen next to last for Lapchick's final tournament. It didn't matter to him because here he was coaching in the town and the building that he loved.

In the last minute of play St. John's had a 2-point lead and started to freeze the ball. Villanova countered with the press. With 10 seconds left and the Redmen still in possession, Villanova, desperate, fouled. Jerry Houston made both fouls and St. John's won, 55–51.

The fans, students and players lifted Joe Lapchick to their shoulders. There was moisture in the old man's eyes. "What a way to go," he said. "What a way to go."

12

ANDY PHILLIP
Whiz Kid

There were two sets of "Whiz Kids" in sporting history, the first competing for the University of Illinois basketball team in the early 1940s, the second competing for baseball's Philadelphia Phillies, National League pennant winners in 1950.

If it hadn't been for Andy Phillip, the nickname never would have developed. Andy Phillip was a 6-3, 195-pound high school star from Granite City, Illinois, who enrolled in the state university in September, 1940, at the same time as three other members of the all-state basketball team. Jack Smiley, Gene Vance and Ken Menke were all fine basketball players. Andy Phillip, however, was the best among them.

Within a year, these four, plus Art Mathisen, not only would electrify a state but a country as well with their devastating fast break and Andy Phillip's scoring and all-around play.

At the time, the present Big Ten Conference was known as the Western Conference. It was the top intercollegiate sports league in the United States with some of the nation's most respected teams. Until World War II, Illinois was the best team in that conference.

When Phillip, Vance, Menke and Smiley were sophomores, in 1941–42, Illinois won 11 straight games. Their exploits were being beamed around the Midwest then by Grayce Howlett, sports director for WGN in Chicago. One night as the Illini were romping past another startled opponent, Howlett exclaimed, in his best dramatic voice, "Gee, those kids really whiz down the floor." The next day, Howlett went on the air with the term "Whiz Kids."

Andy Phillip, the star of that team, had a choice between a baseball career with the St. Louis Cardinals, and a basketball career at Illinois. Ironically, a former Illinois athlete who had become one of the most successful figures in baseball steered Phillip to college and, consequently, to basketball.

The man was Lou Boudreau, the former manager and shortstop for the Cleveland Indians. Boudreau had played baseball and basketball at Illinois and was a well-known figure in the state, constantly in demand for speaking engagements at high school banquets.

In 1938, Lou Boudreau spoke at a dinner in Granite City, Andy Phillip's home town. Andy, who had shown great promise as a baseball player, had already been offered a contract. "I was fifteen then," Phillip said, "and I had always set my sights on playing as well as Lou since seeing him play at Illinois."

After the banquet, Boudreau advised Andy to go to college. "Lou told me, 'You'll never regret it. You'll do well in college, then you'll be able to sign a bigger baseball or basketball contract.' Lou hadn't completed college, but he wanted me not to follow him but to take his advice. I did, and I'll always be happy and proud that I did," Phillip said many years later.

Doug Mills thought Boudreau had given Andy great

advice. And why shouldn't he feel that way? Mills was the basketball coach at Illinois. Andy Phillip made him a famous man.

Phillip was not an immediate success, despite having been talented enough to lead his high school team to the state title the winter before enrolling at Illinois.

"He wasn't a great player then," Mills said. "In fact, Andy had as far to go as did any of the 'Whiz Kids.' Perhaps he needed even more attention, more work, more effort, to perfect his style."

He was a rangy and physically tough youngster whose hands had the delicate feel for great shooting and ballhandling. On the floor, his movements, both on offense and defense could be described as catlike.

By the start of his sophomore year, 1941–42, the little flaws were gone. Illinois won its first game, lost to a star-studded air force team from Chanute Field, 40–38, in the second game and then won 11 straight. The Illini finished with an 18–5 record and won the conference title with a 13–2 mark. But in the NCAA tournament, they lost to Kentucky, 46–44.

Andy Phillip was the most valuable player on that Illinois team. He also made the league all-star team, finishing the season with a 10-point average on 230 points in 23 games. It may not sound like much compared to Wilt Chamberlain's scoring average, but in the early 1940s, few teams were averaging better than 50 points a game.

The next season, the "Whiz Kids" and Phillip really took off, captivating the whole country with their exciting, hustling style. They won the Western Conference title again with a 12–0 record and finished 17–1 for the season.

Andy wound up with 305 points, including a new conference single-game scoring mark of 40 points set against the University of Chicago. His average for the season was a surprising 21.2, and it earned him a consensus All-American berth.

His scoring was only one part of Andy's game. Without his defensive rebounding the Illinois fast break would not have been effective, and without his pinpoint passes a lot of plays would have been unsuccessful. Some years later, the Associated Press would recognize his talents by naming him to the all-time All-American team.

In the spring of 1943, Andy Phillip entered the service. Other members of the "Whiz Kids" followed, and Illinois' hopes for a national championship disappeared. Phillip had entered the Marine Corps, serving in the Pacific as a lieutenant.

At war's end, he, Smiley, Vance and Menke returned to Illinois, where they joined with Fred Green at the start of the 1946–47 season. Was this the year for the "Whiz Kids" or had they left their game in the service? The rust was evident from the beginning. It was still a tough team, but it was not as overpowering as it had been before the war.

The "Whiz Kids" finished second in the Western Conference, and their overall record was a disappointing 14–6. Phillip still managed to make one of the All-American teams even though he scored a career low of 192 points.

The professionals knew that Phillip's low scoring was due to his three years in the service, so when it came time for him to graduate they were waiting with a contract. Phillip signed with the Chicago Stags of the National Basketball League and later played for the Philadelphia Warriors, the Fort Wayne Pistons and Boston Celtics.

He was one of the three players involved in one of the most famous transactions in the history of professional basketball. It happened when the Stags folded before the start of the 1950–51 season. The players were then divided among the teams in the National Basketball Association.

Phillip and Max Zaslofsky were the two most prominent members of the Chicago team. There also was a rookie named Bob Cousy, who had not been chosen. New York, Philadelphia and Boston still had to make their selections. Each wanted Zaslofsky.

The only solution was to place the names in a hat and have a drawing. Ned Irish of the New York Knickerbockers selected first, and when he opened his little slip of paper the grin on his face was the tip about the player he had drawn, Max Zaslofsky.

Eddie Gottlieb then drew Phillip, and Walter Brown of Boston was "left" with Bob Cousy. Irish was overjoyed. Zaslofsky was one of the best scorers in professional basketball and was a four-time All-Star. He also was a native New Yorker.

Gottlieb was happy, too, because Phillip would be the perfect addition to a team that already had Paul Arizin and Joe Fulks. Boston had passed up Cousy in the college draft and now seemed stuck with him. He would, of course, turn out to be the best of the three selections.

Phillip was hardly a disappointment in Philadelphia, although his game had changed by now from that of a scorer to that of a playmaker.

"I'm taking less shots than ever," he said. "It seems to me a pass that will lead to a better shot and an easier basket gets the same results. We're all in this thing together. We're out to reach the playoffs and better ourselves financially. What's the difference who shoots as long as you win?"

Not only was it a treat to watch Phillip on the floor, but it was an experience watching him during time-outs. He was a very superstitious person. "You'll notice," he once said, "that in all the huddles I'll always maneuver so that I get to the left side of the coach. I've always done that with my coaches. Then I always have a tendency to turn to my right on coming down stairs and other places. On the floor, you'll notice that whenever possible I'll turn to my right in going back up court. Of course, in an emergency, I'll go to my left, but it really has to be an emergency."

Andy played in five NBA All-Star games and set single-game assist records with 17 in 1951, when he was with Philadelphia, and 19 in 1954, when he was with Fort Wayne. He led the league in assists with 414 in 1950–51 and 539 in 1951–52, a record at the time. He had 3,759 lifetime assists to rank among the NBA's all-time top ten. During his eleven seasons in pro ball, Andy averaged 9.1 points per game on 6,384 points in 701 games.

During this time he also played minor-league baseball, reaching AAA status as a first baseman. But basketball was his sport. He was the classic team player, forever sacrificing his own shot to set up a teammate, and his coaches realized his value.

His greatest days, however, were those he spent with the Illinois basketball team when the "Whiz Kids" sped down the floor, fast-breaking their opponents to defeat.

...

13

HENRY IBA
The Fundamentalist

The young ladies wore miniskirts. Men landed on the
moon. Boys wore their hair longer than the girls. The
Monkey, not the Lindy, was the big dance. Kids lis-
tened to Simon and Garfunkel, not Glenn Miller.

The college generation was known for trying anything new. There were, of course, a few exceptions.
Like at Oklahoma State University. Maybe the majority of students were experimenting and changing, but in
the fieldhouse where Henry Iba ruled, everything was
exactly the same as it was in 1934, when he first arrived at what then was known as Oklahoma A&M.

From the very beginning, Henry Iba preached ball-
control and tight defense. At the end of his career, he
would be preaching the same sermon. Old Henry
should have been an anachronism in 1950, only nobody bothered to tell him.

In the fall of 1968, Iba took a trip, at the request of
the United States Olympic Committee, to Mexico City,
where he coached his second consecutive Olympic basketball champion. Not bad for the master of the ar-
chaic.

After the Olympics, Henry Iba went right back to Stillwater, Oklahoma, and began his thirty-fifth year as head coach at Oklahoma State (the name had been changed a few years before).

He had already won 741 games and lost only 313 as a collegiate coach at Oklahoma State, the University of Colorado and Maryville (Missouri) Teachers College. Among those 741 victories were back-to-back national championships in 1944–45 and 1945–46, fourteen Missouri Valley Conference titles and one Big Eight Conference championship.

His greatest coaching feat, however, may have been with the 1968 Olympic team, hardly a mediocre team, but not on a par with some of the powerhouses the United States had fielded in previous years. "We read among other things that we were a 'smorgasboard' team," said captain Mike Silliman, a team member from the Armed Services. "Every time we picked up a newspaper, we saw ourselves referred to as second-raters. We resented it."

Iba had been critical of All-Americans Elvin Hayes, Lew Alcindor and Westley Unseld for not accepting invitations to the Olympic trials, but he did not use their absence as an excuse or alibi. He knew the team was weaker than the last one he had coached in Tokyo in 1964, and he knew it would face a stiff challenge from Russia, Yugoslavia and Brazil.

With Alcindor, Hayes and Unseld unavailable, the Olympic Committee went about choosing a team. Again, there was a barrage of criticism directed at both the committee and Iba because such outstanding shooters and "name" players as Calvin Murphy of Niagara, Rick Mount of Purdue and Pete Maravich of Louisiana State were not selected.

Instead, the Committee chose such "unknowns" as Spencer Haywood from Trinity (Colorado) Jr. College,

Calvin Fowler and Mike Silliman, the former West Point star, from the U.S. Army and teamed them with a group of less famed collegiate players such as Jo Jo White from Kansas, Ken Spain of Houston, Charlie Scott of North Carolina and Bill Hosket of Ohio State.

The Committee knew this was Iba's type of team: unselfish players with many talents who would play defense and deliberate basketball—basketball the way Iba coached it. Iba molded the team the same way he molded his teams from Oklahoma State. They practiced fundamentals and adhered to the most minute details. Iba worked long and hard with his Olympians before the Games, and when his team defeated the professional New York Knickerbockers in Madison Square Garden in the fall of 1968, the public and the basketball world knew he had done another fine coaching job.

Then came the Games, and, surprisingly, the United States had little trouble winning the gold medal. Puerto Rico, which lost a 61–56 decision to the U.S., provided the toughest test. In the title game, Iba's team defeated Yugoslavia, 65–50.

"This club," Iba said, smiling, when it was all over, "has come a long way in a short time. They've got a lot of pride. If they didn't, we might have been out of this a long time ago."

What was it about Iba and his methods, surely considered outdated and even backward in 1968, that enabled his Olympic team—and his college teams—to win so easily and so often?

Lucious Jackson, one of his former pupils on the 1964 Olympic team, provided the most succinct answer about the man and his philosophy. "I really learned from him," said Jackson, who went on to star in the National Basketball Association for Philadelphia. "He gets on one thing and he stresses that point until everyone knows it. It doesn't matter if it's offense or defense. You have to learn it.

"Before our third game in the Olympics he had made us hand in our playbooks and go to our rooms. He told us to diagram every play and turn them in to him. That's what I mean about making sure you learn everything. I suppose that's why his teams at Oklahoma State play such deliberate ball. When they're on offense they have the plays down so well they can just wait for the good opportunity.

"Defensively, he just told us we wouldn't win if we didn't play it right. He said it was the key, and everybody knew it. He started with a few fundamentals and worked from there. It turned out he was right."

It is hard to envision Iba as anything but a basketball coach. In college, though, he had ideas about being a dentist, but the idea vanished quickly. Born in Easton, Missouri, Aug. 6, 1904, Iba developed into an all-around athlete in grade school and high school. He enrolled at Westminster College, Fulton, Missouri, and played football, basketball and baseball. He received his degree from Northwest State Teachers College in Maryville, also in Missouri.

Following graduation, he coached the Classen High School team in Oklahoma City for three years, then returned to Maryville, where his teams won 101 games and lost only 14.

At that time the National AAU Tournament was the only post-season championship, and Maryville went to the finals only to lose to the famed Henry Clothiers of Wichita by 1 point.

That was Iba's first taste of national tournament play, but it would not be his last. After spending one year at the University of Colorado, Iba accepted the job as basketball coach at Oklahoma A&M in 1934.

Ball-control was the style in the '30s. A team patiently worked and maneuvered for the one clear shot that would give it a good chance for 2 points. The ball was like gold. One didn't throw it away on frivolities.

This made good sense to Iba. It continued to make sense even when the game began to change. Iba claims he decided to stick with the controlled, patterned, defensive game because, "I was taught that you never should let a boy get beaten badly. And that's why we use the system we do. When a boy gets beaten badly, he has a long hill to climb before he's ready to play well. The way the game is built, if you score, I get the ball. If I score, you get it. That makes it a matter of eliminating mistakes.

"You ought to be able to control the tempo of the game with the proper self-discipline. You're not always successful, but you should be. If you control the tempo, the chances of your getting beat by 30 points are considerably smaller—even if you're up against a vastly superior opponent."

Iba's basketball infuriated many of his fellow coaches, who usually wound up frustrated losers after tangling with the Cowpokes. The opposition invented many nicknames for Iba's teams, like the "Slowpokes." One coach always referred to his road games against Oklahoma A&M as being played in "Stallwater."

Jack Gray, the former coach at the University of Texas, sought legislation for a time limit such as the professionals adopted in the 1950s. The rule would require the offensive team to shoot within a set amount of time. Henry Iba and Oklahoma A&M were the reasons for Gray's proposal.

"The Oklahoma City Tournament (1950) was one of the dullest you ever saw, principally because there were five ball-control teams in the tournament. Iba had his team there and they won it," Gray said.

"Sure, ball-control his its place, but I think too many

teams are adopting this style of basketball and I expect to see legislation soon. After all, the game is for the fans, and they like to see plenty of scoring, just as in football."

Iba had heard it all before. He did not change. His teams primarily played a man-for-man defense, but during the Bob Kurland era at Oklahoma A&M, the Cowpokes played a semi-zone. Kurland, one of the game's first 7-footers, was stationed in front of the basket, and whenever the opposition would shoot he would try to bat the ball away from the basket.

It worked often enough and finally the National Collegiate Athletic Association had to pass a rule barring goaltending.

The goaltending rule did not hamper Kurland or Oklahoma A&M. The three-time All-American went on to lead his team to the national championship two straight seasons, marking the first time that had been done. The first championship came by defeating NYU, 49–45; the second was capped by a 43–40 victory over North Carolina. In 1948–49, the year Iba was voted coach of the year, Oklahoma lost a 43–36 decision to Kentucky in the finals.

By that time the game was changing rapidly. Different shooting styles, taller players, new rules, improved coaching methods, all played a part. Iba, however, stubbornly held to his ball-control views. "All in all," he said before heading for Tokyo in 1964, "the game has progressed very well. I think every rule change has been a good one."

The biggest change, he claimed, was the quality and consistency of the shooters. "A few years ago," he said, "you thought you had a couple of boys who could hit 40 percent of their shots from the field. Today, you have six or seven men on a club who can shoot that well."

Iba had some fine shooters at Oklahoma State, and his 1964 Olympic team was one of the best groups of basketball players ever assembled. Among the Olympians were Jackson, Bill Bradley, Jeff Mullins, Walt Hazzard, Joe Caldwell, Mel Counts and Larry Brown, who later became stars in the professional leagues.

"I'm not against shooting," Iba often said. "I'm against bad shooting. I want my boys to shoot. I love my boys to shoot. But, glory be, make it a good shot."

Iba had a pair of deep-set eyes and a leathery, deeply lined face that expressed utter horror at a bad play on the floor. "I've seen him cringe," said his assistant, Sam Aubrey, "when the *other* team made a mistake."

Somehow, Iba's gray hair, with the part in the middle, told the story of the man. He was of another era, but was smart enough to compete in the modern one, too. Whenever he and his teams appeared, Iba was always ready to defend his style of play. "An awful lot of people give lip-service to defense in basketball," he said, "but we work at it in Stillwater. Here is our chief contention—airtight defense will get you a win more often than a high-geared offense. The point is this: I don't care how good some 'shooting' team is, the offense of that club will fluctuate by a much wider margin than will a defense as good as ours ordinarily is. Why, some variations will amount to as much as 10 or 15 points per night. It's even more so now than in the past because teams are losing the ball a lot more these days (1960s). That's due to the change in the game. We don't have passers anymore.

"On our poor nights we figure our defense will carry us. Consistency is our main theme, and we like to think that our game develops a clear, methodical kind of thinker. Our man has a good reason for everything he does on that court. He does nothing on impulse; he follows his mind's good reasoning. Here is our prevailing motto: 'Think and then act. Never act, and then alibi.' "

Perhaps Iba's most memorable demonstration of his ball-control and defense tactics came during the 1948–1949 season. Oklahoma A&M was matched against the unbeaten team from St. Louis University, which had All-American Ed Macauley in the lineup.

The critics claimed that Iba and his team set the sport back twenty years by winning, 29–27. When it was over, however, Iba smiled, winked his eye and added another digit in the win column. It wasn't very artistic, but it was successful. That is an adequate description of Henry Iba's career.

14

JOHN WOODEN
India Rubber Man

UCLA was 2 minutes away from winning its historic third straight national collegiate basketball championship when Bruin coach John Wooden stood up and began walking in front of his team's bench, pausing for a moment to converse with each player.

"I told them," Wooden said, "that I was proud of the fact we have won national titles before and the players haven't gone haywire immediately after. I told them I saw no reason for excessive jubilation. I think that's the best way to feel. I don't think winning a game means that much and I don't think losing does either."

That was the mood in Louisville's Freedom Hall, March 22, 1969, the day John Wooden became the first coach to win five national titles and the day his team became the first in history to win three straight championships by defeating Wooden's alma mater, Purdue, 92–72.

John Wooden, an uncomplicated man of Midwestern virtue, had lived for many years in the hip, cool-as-ice, fast-moving world of Southern California. The land did not convert John Wooden. Nor did John Wooden convert the land. It was an uneasy standoff.

Wooden, during the years of his greatest success—1964 through 1969—had many detractors, some on his UCLA basketball team, who considered him a fossil from a prehistoric world. There were others who looked at the man's accomplishments and concluded that he was the greatest coach in a game that produced Red Auerbach, Adolph Rupp, Henry Iba, Joe Lapchick, Phog Allen and Nat Holman, among others.

A very quiet, very precise man, Wooden disarmed people who probed too far with a warm smile while actually telling them no. He reminded many people of a country parson who chased the devil from under every rock in the village.

His shell-rimmed glasses, long pointed nose and thin lips added to an image that was not entirely inaccurate. Wooden was born October 14, 1910, and raised on a farm 8 miles from Martinsville, Indiana. And though he had moved from there many years earlier, he was still very much the country boy during his coaching years at UCLA.

When he was mildly angry, he would rebuke his players with a "Gracious sakes alive." When he was very angry it would be "Goodness gracious sakes alive." It was becoming decorum for a deacon of the First Christian Church of Santa Monica, California.

Wooden was strict with his players in a paternalistic sense. He tolerated no smoking or drinking or profanity, abstaining from all three himself. He was devotee of conditioning and told each player on the first day of practice, "Take care of your health—mental, moral and physical. Force yourself to keep running and working hard when you're tired in order to improve your condition."

Wooden also devised what he called the Pyramid of

Success chart and distributed it to his players. The pyramid is built on fifteen blocks labeled *industriousness, friendship, loyalty, cooperation, enthusiasm, self-control, alertness, initiative, intentness, condition, skill, team spirit, poise, confidence* and *competitive greatness.*

The blocks were held together by ten other intangibles: *ambition, adaptability, resourcefulness, fight, fate, sincerity, honesty, integrity, reliability* and *patience.*

The pyramid made Wooden one of the most successful coaches in history. First there were the five national titles within six years; his teams also had 21 consecutive winning seasons. There were countless Coach of the Year awards, including three national awards, 1963–64, 1966–67 and 1968–69. For 33 years, through the 1969 season, his combined high school and college coaching record was 714–193.

He was the only coach whose teams twice had 30–0 seasons. UCLA did it in 1963–64 and again in 1966–67. In 1966, a 7-1 center from New York City named Lew Alcindor joined Wooden's varsity team and for the next three seasons the Bruins were national champions. During that time they won 88 of 90 games, losing only to the University of Houston (1967–68) and the University of Southern California (1968–69), each time by 2 points.

John Wooden's basketball success was not limited to coaching. He was one of the greatest all-around guards to play the game of basketball, and his years spent at this position shaped his philosophy of the game. Until Alcindor joined his team, Wooden never had a squad with an outstanding big man.

Wooden, 5-10, was a brilliant defensive player and an outstanding scorer—for the times—while at Purdue. He played the game with a lot of determination and earned the nickname the "India Rubber Man" because he was always bouncing off the floor.

He was a three-time All-American from 1930 through 1932. In 1932 he was chosen Player of the Year. That same year, Purdue was selected as the national basketball champion.

Teammate Dutch Fehring, who later taught at Stanford, remembered Wooden as a collegian. "He had a way of stalling the game by fantastic dribbling," Fehring said. "He would dribble from backcourt to forecourt, all around, and nobody could get that ball away."

At the time John Wooden was playing for Purdue, Tom Harmon, who later became a football hero, was a schoolboy in Gary, Indiana, and was a John Wooden fan. "Wooden, to the kids of my era, was what Bill Russell, Wilt Chamberlain or Lew Alcindor is today. He was king, the idol of any kid who had a basketball. And in Indiana that was every kid," Harmon said.

Wooden's defensive play helped Purdue set a number of records. In ten conference games during the 1929–30 season, Purdue opponents scored only 215 points; in 1930–31 it was only 275 points in twelve games; and in 1931–32 it was 303 points in twelve games. During that 1931–32 season he set a scoring record for the Western Conference with 154 points in twelve games. That was the equivalent of scoring 25 per game in modern play.

It is not surprising, then, that Wooden's trademark at UCLA was defense. He was considered the originator of the full-court zone press, which helped revolutionize the game of basketball in the 1960s. The zone press became an integral part of the UCLA program, which also featured a devastating fast break, a patterned offense and tight man-to-man defense. UCLA's ability to switch defenses quickly and efficiently demoralized many of its opponents.

Wooden was always a respected figure in basketball, but he became one of the game's giants when his teams started winning national championships in the mid 1960s. The first national title came in 1963–64 and was followed by the second a year later. The Bruins didn't win it in 1965–66, but the following season, Alcindor's first with the varsity, they defeated Dayton for the title. The Bruins defeated the University of North Carolina for the 1967–68 title and broke the record by defeating Purdue in 1968–69.

"This team," Wooden said before UCLA won its third straight and fifth national championship, "is a quiet team except for an individual or two. It's not a team that shows a lot of emotion. Part of my philosophy is that I don't want any undue dejection when we lose or any undue celebration when we win."

Wooden was like his team. He occasionally berated the officials during a game, but most of the time he sat primly on the bench, seldom rising from his seat. He often applauded like a fan for a well-executed play.

His emotions always were well-masked, but before the championship game in 1968–69, he cracked slightly and admitted that game was one of the most important of his life. "It's not so much for me," he said. "For a coach, the first national championship is the most important. But no team has ever won three straight, and I would like to see our seniors have three in a row. I think it will be a long time before that happens again, and I would like these players to share that distinction."

The Alcindor era was one of the most exciting in the history of basketball. And sometimes the pressure on the youngster, on the team and on the coach was unbearable. The team was not supposed to lose. "Once you're No. 1," Wooden said, "people are never satisfied with anything less. I'm not crying. I'm just saying what it's like."

The years also were turbulent—off the basketball court. Campuses, including UCLA's, were the scene of much social change with black students at the center of this turmoil. Alcindor was an extremely intelligent young man concerned with the times and there were numerous reports that he, as well as some of his team-mates, did not really get along with Wooden, who was branded as a dogmatic coach and man.

Wooden later said, "The Alcindor era has been a tremendous era for basketball. But this has not been as easy an era for UCLA as it seems to be to outsiders. This," he added, referring to the 1968–69 season, "has been my most trying year in coaching. I've talked with a number of coaches who have said the same thing. The problems are not reduced to basketball only. Lots of things are changing. Modes of dress, speech, ideas. Life is more hectic for everyone from the President on down.

"We coaches must change, too, and I think we are. But with all the change the underlying philosophy of the coach must remain the same. I've tried to face these problems rather than ignore them. They're there and we need more tolerance with those who have different ideas."

If there was a lot of pressure on the team and Wood-en, there was even more on Alcindor, who, according to Wooden, was the greatest player in the history of collegiate basketball.

"This boy," he said, "was in the most unique position of any athlete in the history of sports. You have no idea of the demands on him. For a number of weeks during his senior year, a day did not go by when I didn't get a long-distance call from lawyers, tax men, accountants, agents. They all said they wanted to repre-sent him. But they didn't really want to handle Lewis. They wanted to handle what he could bring in."

Alcindor eventually signed with Milwaukee of the National Basketball Association for a reported $1.4-million package.

There were times when Wooden seemed to wish he were back in Martinsville, where life was much quieter and much easier to comprehend. And he seemed relieved when the Alcindor era ended. "It will be nice," he said, "to get back where I'm coaching to win instead of coaching not to lose."

Wooden showed the basketball world some of its finest coaching—during the Alcindor years and earlier. "Wooden's success," said one of his rival coaches, "is based on upsetting the tempo and style of his opponent. He does it by running, and running some more. He mixes that up by hawking, by grabbing, by slapping and by a hand-waving defense. His clubs dote on harassing the man with the ball."

It is an accurate analysis, and that style of play made Wooden as famous a coach as he was a player. During his time, UCLA became synonymous with excellence. The public flocked to watch his teams, and during a two-season period, 1966–68, UCLA attracted 765,571 fans.

In 1965, UCLA began playing its home games in a beautiful $5-million arena named Pauley Pavilion. Its seating capacity was 12,800. Shortly after the opening of the building, some friends from Martinsville visited the Woodens in Los Angeles. The UCLA coach showed them Pauley Pavilion.

They sat down in the deep theater seats and stared out at the gleaming floor and the banners proclaiming UCLA's basketball accomplishments. "John," said his friend Floyd Burns. "It sure is a long way from Martinsville to all this."

John Wooden smiled and shook his head in agreement.

15

ADOLPH RUPP
The Baron

He carried the nickname of "The Baron." Few have been so aptly named. Adolph Frederick Rupp raised prize cattle, choice tobacco and talented basketball players. And just as in bygone days, he ran each business like a fiefdom. "Nobody," Adolph Rupp once stated, "talks back to me."

That was the man's philosophy, and it made him the winningest college basketball coach of all time. It was not a popular philosophy, nor was Adolph Rupp a popular man. His iron fist was his scepter, and some came to fear it, some to respect it and many to despise it.

"To sit by and worry about criticism, which too often comes from the misinformed or from those incapable of passing judgment on an individual or a problem, is a waste of time," Rupp said. "I've gotten a lot of publicity for being a mean man. But it's not true. The fact is that I've got an invitation to coach both basketball teams when I go through the pearly gates."

It is unfortunate that criticism and controversy so shrouded the career of Adolph Rupp, who made winning basketball at the University of Kentucky as much a tradition in the Bluegrass country as the Kentucky Derby. But the controversy is an integral part of the man and the man's story because he caused it and, at times, seemed to use it as a strategic weapon in the one battle that meant something to him—winning a basketball game.

The list of Rupp's basketball achievements are unending. When he was sixty-seven, in his thirty-ninth year of coaching at Kentucky, his team won its 800th game. His winning percentage over all those years was an incredible .822. No other college coach came close to matching it. Rupp was national Coach of the Year four times and runner-up two other seasons. In 1967, the Columbus, Ohio, Touchdown Club honored him as the "Coach of the Century."

His Kentucky teams won four National Collegiate championships, appeared in more national tournaments (eighteen) than any other collegiate team and claimed more victories in championship-tournament play (27) than any other team. Rupp also coached the 1948 Olympic champions, a team that included members of his Kentucky NCAA champions. He has produced more Olympic gold-medal winners (seven) in basketball than any other coach.

He also has developed more All-Americans (24 players honored 34 times) and more professional players (26) than any other coach. "Rupp-trained players," said Red Auerbach, then coach and general manager of the Boston Celtics, "are better grounded in the fundamentals than any others." Rupp's teams also have won 24 Southeastern Conference championships, five Sugar Bowl Tournament championships, one National Invitation Tournament championship and eleven University of Kentucky Invitational championships.

"It's fundamentals," Rupp said. "It's the work we

give them in the fundamentals, there's no other way. The first thing you have to do is curtail the individual desire of the boy in the interest of team play. Then you have to correct two deficiencies every boy has—in playing defense and in recognizing the value of ball-possession."

Through the years, Rupp was a strong proponent of man-to-man defense. It wasn't until late in his career that he began using a zone defense. "Don't get me wrong," he said. "I'm still not an advocate of the zone. The zone, to my way of thinking, has two weaknesses. It still won't come close to getting the job done against the many excellent shooting teams we have these days. In man-to-man play, you harass the shooter and hope he cools off. With most zones, the hot shooter simply shoots over it without being annoyed too much."

Rupp was a traditionalist. Hs teams didn't vary much from year to year in their style of play. "At Kentucky," he was fond of saying, "it's traditional with us to start out with two things: The National Anthem and a guard-around play I've been calling Number 6 as long as I can remember. This lets us know immediately if an opponent is using a zone against us, and we can adjust immediately."

Speed and finesse were Kentucky trademarks, and when things were going right a Kentucky team was a beautiful sight. Bob Cousy, the great professional, once remarked, "I'd rather watch Kentucky practice than watch most teams play."

Kentucky's reputation was more imposing than its won-lost record. "Every team," Rupp said proudly, "is out for Kentucky's skin. We are their big game of the year. We can't point for every game on our schedule, but we never play a team that isn't pointing for us."

Adolph Rupp was born in Halstead, Kansas, Sept. 2, 1901. He attended the University of Kansas and played guard for one of the all-time great coaches, Phog Allen. He was graduated in 1923, coached high school basketball in Marshalltown, Iowa, and Freeport, Illinois, then, in 1930, arrived at the University of Kentucky.

Many years later, Rupp could look back and say, "We here at the University of Kentucky are fortunate. We have a great basketball tradition. Almost every boy in this area lives for the day when he can come to the University of Kentucky and represent it on the basketball floor. We don't have to recruit. . . . We've got the best place to play. No sir, the kids write to us. Why, we got 500 letters of application (one year) . . . you can't beat that setup. I guess we get more boys on scholarships than any team in the country. All a kid has to do is tell a coach he's got an offer from Kentucky. The coach will never check. He's quick to offer the boy one from his own school."

It was a dynasty, all right, and Rupp ruled like a monarch. His practices were long and they were hard, and above all they were silent. "It is generally understood out there," Rupp explained, "that no one is to speak unless he can improve on the silence. . . . Why should boys constantly chatter in a class in basketball any more than they do in a class in English?

"They say I'm hard on kids. Whenever I win something the first thing they say is 'Rupp drives his team to victory.' With anybody else they'd say, 'So-and-so leads his team to victory.' They just don't let themselves give me full credit. Well, that's the difference. Of course you drive a team. Somebody has to be behind them. And as far as character-building goes, you build more character by winning than you do by losing. Don't forget that. And they say it's no fun to play for me. How silly can you get? What's more fun than winning?

"Basketball," he continued, "is a game of rhythm. The only way you're going to get that rhythm is by repetition. You do a thing thousands of times and pretty soon you do it easily and gracefully. That's the way my boys put the ball in the basket. They practice everything so much there's no stuttering around during a game. They move and they know where they're moving and why they're moving. Personally, I think it's a damn good system."

Rupp had his problems through the years with players who tired of his methods and rebelled. When each incident became public, as in the cases of Linville Puckett, Bob Tallent and Greg Starrick, it caused a sensation in Kentucky. But during all his trials and hard times, the fans of Kentucky remained solidly behind "the man in the Brown suit." (Wearing a brown suit to his team's games was a Rupp trademark.)

In 1955, three years after the most controversial, most publicized part of Rupp's career, 12,500 fans jammed Memorial Coliseum in Lexington for a game between Kentucky and Tennessee. The game was only secondary, for that night the good people of Kentucky were helping Adolph Rupp celebrate his Silver Anniversary at the University. His gift from the state's appreciative fans was a Cadillac.

In many ways the Cadillac was the perfect symbol for Rupp, for by now he had become a rich, powerful man as much renowned for his white-faced Herefords as his winning basketball teams. There was no doubting his talent as a coach, but there still was much doubt concerning his methods. Most of that doubt came from outside the state of Kentucky.

Rupp, like many coaches past and present, viewed himself as more than a coach. "Evangelist" would be a fitting term. Rupp spread the gospel of discipline, virtue and self-sacrifice through the provinces. Much of what he preached was true. Very often, however, Rupp did not seem to listen to his own sermons.

No biography of Adolph Rupp would be complete without examining those unforgettable days of the early 1950s, when the point-shaving scandals swept college basketball and nearly destroyed it. Many coaches and players saw their careers and lives broken by it. Adolph Rupp survived, and eventually grew stronger.

It was August 1951, and Rupp was in Lincoln, Nebraska. "Gamblers," he said, "couldn't get at our players with a 10-foot pole." Adolph Rupp was wrong. The gamblers had reached his players: Alex Groza, Ralph Beard, Dale Barnstable, Jim Line and Walter Hirsch; Bill Spivey, the 7-foot center, was also implicated. But it was never proved that he was involved in point-shaving.

The investigation at Kentucky went much deeper than gambling. It embraced the whole basketball program, and when the investigation was concluded, New York judge Saul Streit, under whose auspices the investigation had been conducted, delivered a stinging rebuke against Rupp and the University. In a 63-page statement, the judge charged Rupp, the University and the townspeople with overemphasizing the basketball program. He concluded his report by saying, "The University and coach must share the responsibility with the fixers for corrupting and demoralizing these defendants."

In November 1952 the NCAA placed Kentucky on probation for one year for having violated subsidization and eligibility rules. The school then announced it would cancel the 1952–53 basketball schedule. Would Rupp stay on as coach? "I had planned to retire with the 'Fabulous Five' (the 1948–49 team of Beard, Groza, Wah Wah Jones, Kenny Rollins and Cliff Barker), but they had the Coliseum coming along and there was great need for good teams to fill the house," Rupp said. "I felt it was my duty to stay on. The boys needed me worse than ever and it would have looked awfully bad if I had walked out on the heels of this thing."

Many people in basketball felt that Adolph Rupp's greatest achievement came during the 1953–54 season, when Kentucky resumed its schedule. That was the team led by Cliff Hagan, Frank Ramsey and Lou Tsioropoulos. The Wildcats took every advantage of an emotional situation and won all 25 games on the schedule, but they did not compete in the NCAA tournament, because some players had completed work for their degrees and were ineligible for postseason play. Rupp called that team "the best I have ever seen," adding, "I have coached four other teams that were rated national champions, but this team was superior to all four. It ran through an undefeated season and never was extended." La Salle, which won the national title that season, lost to Kentucky during the regular campaign by 13 points.

Rupp and the state felt vindicated, and Kentucky basketball remained in the same spot it had occupied before the trouble. Then, in 1957–58, Kentucky enjoyed another memorable season. This time the situation was much different. The Wildcats lost 6 games during the regular season, more than any Kentucky team had lost in a regular season for seventeen years. Also, not one Kentucky player had been selected on so much as an all-conference team prior to the NCAA tournament.

The first five on that team consisted of Vern Hatton, Johnny Cox, John Crigler, Adrian Smith and Ed Beck. Kentucky reached the final round of the tournament by defeating Miami (Ohio) and Notre Dame in the regionals, and then in a semifinal game defeated Temple,

61–60. In the title game, the Wildcats defeated Seattle, 84–72.

As the years passed and Adolph Rupp's jowls and waistline grew, much of the bitterness surrounding him began to dissolve. He was growing old, and though he remained as difficult and demanding as always, he also began to mellow. Besides, the Wildcats were not quite as unbeatable as in earlier years. There were 19–9, 16–9 and 15–10 records during the 1960s. Then in 1965–66 came what seemed like Rupp's last chance for a national championship, and once again the emotion swirled around him, and again a state and a nation found themselves captivated by a Kentucky basketball team.

This team was special to Rupp and the fans because it did not have a starter taller than 6-5. The team's nickname was "Rupp's Runts." It was Rupp's sentimental favorite. "He has fallen in love with this club as with none other," said Rupp's longtime assistant, Harry Lancaster.

The season before (1964–65) had been Rupp's worst since coming to Kentucky. His team finished 15–10, which by normal standards is not bad. In Kentucky, however, it is considered a disaster. The experts predicted another frustrating season for Kentucky in 1965–66. Again they were wrong. The team, consisting of Pat Riley, Lou Dampier, Larry Conley, Thad Jaracz and Tommy Kron, hustled its way to a 24–1 record during regular-season play.

Victories over Dayton, Michigan and Duke moved the Wildcats into the final against Texas Western and a chance at a fifth national title. Rupp and his team did not get it. The Miners won, 72–65. When it was over, Adolph Rupp was a sad, tired old man in a rumpled brown suit. Even though Kentucky lost in the finals, Rupp's old adversaries, the writers, recognized the magnificent job of coaching and named him Coach of the Year.

Wherever Adolph Rupp went his presence stirred controversy and interest. For many he was the Elmer Gantry of basketball. To others he was the greatest figure in the game. There is no arguing with his record. It will stand for a long time, and few will forget the great national-championship teams he produced in 1948, 1949, 1951 and 1958.

Nor will they forget the names of Ralph Beard, Alex Groza, Cliff Hagan, Frank Ramsey, Bill Spivey, Wah Wah Jones, Lou Tsioropoulos, Johnny Cox, Adrian Smith, Cotton Nash, Pat Riley and Lou Dampier. They were Adolph Rupp's boys, the ones who made him the greatest collegiate coach in basketball. He drove them hard every minute, and the record book is proof that his methods were successful.

"Tradition," Rupp said, "is important. It carries on from year to year. Boys will emulate and copy the style of play that has been used by those who have gone before. Our boys, during the course of the year, will look for hours at moving pictures of our great athletes in order to copy and learn the best methods of executing our fundamental details. It is not necessary for us to do a big selling job to our boys. Spirit is contagious—and if we can create within the boys a genuine desire to give the best they have at all times, then I am sure the best will come back to us.

"We do not wish merely to participate in sports. We wish to be successful in sports. In order to be successful we must create within these boys the competitive spirit that will bring success. Defeat and failure to me are enemies. Without victory, basketball has little meaning. I would not give one iota to make the trip from the cradle to the grave unless I could live in a competitive world.

"Success bolsters the individual morale and the morale of the entire student body, and I do not belive anything has happened in the Commonwealth of Kentucky which has given so much genuine joy and satisfaction as the University team winning the NCAA tournament in 1958. Success is the cement that holds people or organizations together."

Nobody, including a long line of governors and other politicians, had such a dramatic influence on the state of Kentucky as Adolph Rupp did when his Wildcats, in their blue and white uniforms, ran onto the basketball floor.

16

RED AUERBACH
Compassionate Dictator

It was one of the great rituals in sport. The scoreboard clock would be clicking away 00:04 . . . 00:03 . . . 00:02 . . . and Red Auerbach would reach in his pocket for a match and the cigar that meant the Boston Celtics had won another basketball game. Through the years, the cigar-lighting ceremony began to assume new dimensions, especially in cities such as St. Louis and Philadelphia, where losing to Boston was not appreciated. There the cigar became a symbol of a city's frustration—a symbol of hatred. A symbol that constantly reminded those who would challenge that they were not good enough—they were second best.

Arnold Auerbach smoked a lot of cigars during his twenty seasons in the National Basketball Association. At the end, April 28, 1966, there were 1,037 victories and 548 defeats. There were also nine world's championships, eight in succession beginning in 1959 and stretching through 1966.

There were many aspects of Auerbach's career besides victories and cigars. There were battles with officials, both game officials and league officials; there were fines, more than $17,000 worth; there were tirades against and fights with spectators; but most important, there were ten, sometimes eleven or twelve, men in kelly green uniforms who believed in and gave complete respect to the balding man with the roled-up program in his hand.

Red Auerbach was a lot of things. He admittedly was an egotist. He also, again admittedly, was a dictator. "A dictator with compassion," was his favorite description. To this he added an overwhelming knowledge of his game plus an understanding of the motivations of the American male athlete. His were the greatest, the most powerful, the most polished teams in the history of basketball, the teams that turned the sport into an art.

Through the years there have been theories and explanations for Red Auerbach's success. Millions of words have been written about him. He has written books and articles about the game, he has given countless clinics, but somehow it all seems to come down to this one Auerbach sentence: "Strategy is something anyone can learn. But not all coaches take the time to understand a man's personality."

Red Auerbach was a "compassionate" dictator. There have been other coaches in the game, indeed other coaches in the Hall of Fame, who were winners because they were autocrats. They could not even remember their players' names. Auerbach was not that type of man. He was strict, yes, but he cared, and he blended the two philosophies perfectly.

"I'll help my players in business, in private investment, publicitywise, but I won't drink beer with them while they play for me," he said. "A coach can't play cards, share a room or socialize with his players if he expects to be a success in the pro game. He can be friendly, yes. He can eat or go to the movies with his squad occasionally when the team is on the road. He can even buy a present for a man's new baby. But there has to be a stop point. My players know what it is."

Every team he coached knew that point, knew it well. And it never tried to break the unwritten rules. In the end, his teams benefited. Not only were they the best, they were the richest and most respected.

Perhaps the first clue to Red Auerbach's future success centered around an incident in 1936, when he won a scholarship to George Washington University in Washington, D.C. As a youngster in the Williamsburg section of Brooklyn, he had pressed pants in his father's dry-cleaning store. His basketball, during that time, consisted of games on the local playgrounds and the rooftop court of Public School 122. He was not an outstanding player, but he was talented and determined.

When he arrived at George Washington he found himself competing with five others for the one guard position still open. "I had four fistfights in the first two weeks of practice," Auerbach said. "I got the job." Auerbach was 5-foot-10 and his problem was speed. At Seth Low Junior College, where he had matriculated before attending George Washington, he tried to correct a deficiency that seemed uncorrectable.

"Hour after hour . . . in some airless gym or in the school playgrounds . . . I worked on starts and stops, ran sideways and backwards and drove at full speed from one end of the court to the other until I was ready to fall down," Auerbach said.

"I kept at it day after day, every day, because I was convinced that through proper application you could make your body do a good deal more than it seemed capable of doing. I took this conviction all through my career, both as an athlete and a coach."

Coaching stints at St. Albans Prep and Roosevelt

High School in Washington followed Auerbach's graduation from George Washington. Then came World War II and Arnold Auerbach found himself an officer in the United States Navy. He spent most of his service time at the naval base in Norfolk, Virginia.

In 1946, still in the Navy, Auerbach learned that a group of men planned to form a professional basketball league. They planned a franchise for Washington. Auerbach's coaching experience may have been limited to high school and military basketball, but it didn't deter him from seeking out Mike Uline, who was to operate the Washington franchise. Auerbach, though an unknown, proved that he also had a keen business mind. He told the Washington owner that it would be extremely difficult competing financially against the larger cities, which had the larger arenas, for the name college stars. Auerbach told Uline he knew a number of fine ballplayers at the Norfolk Naval Base who would be interested in playing professional basketball after their military duty expired. Auerbach then gave him a few facts and figures about the players he had in mind, told Uline about the record they had compiled at Norfolk and then broke into a grin when Uline told him, "You've got the job. I'll give you a one-year contract for $5,000."

Auerbach's team in the Basketball Association of America had a 49–11 record that first year, finishing first in the Eastern Division, but losing in the first round of the playoffs to the Chicago Stags. The mainstays of that team were people like Bob Feerick, Fat Freddie Scolari, Bones McKinney and Johnny Norlander. Auerbach remained with the Capitols for three seasons before moving to Ben Kerner's Tri-Cities franchise during the 1949–50 season.

Kerner, as much an individualist as Auerbach, angered his coach by trading John Mahnken, one of

Auerbach's better ballplayers. Kerner did not bother to consult his coach. The irate Auerbach quit and returned to his home in Washington wondering whether he should seek another coaching job or look for a position as a schoolteacher.

In Boston, Walter Brown and Lou Pieri had just bought the Celtics, a team that had finished in last place the year before. Boston was looking for a new coach and Auerbach's name had been mentioned. The Boston owners called Auerbach and offered him a one-year contract at $10,000, which Auerbach accepted. The Celtics finished with a 39–30 record that season (1950–51), 2½ games out of first place, and from that point Red Auerbach's future was certain. The Boston Celtics would be his team.

Bob Cousy and Ed Macauley were two of the players on Auerbach's first Boston team. Ironically, Auerbach almost lost Cousy. In the spring of 1950, Cousy was among the college stars eligible for the NBA draft. Auerbach, who had just assumed his new duties, did not seem interested in the little backcourt man. He wanted a rebounder, a center, and thought he had his man in Chuck Share, the 6-11 center from Bowling Green. When asked about his plans for the draft, Auerbach told a group of reporters, "Do you want me to get together a basketball team, or do you want me to satisfy the local yokels?" Cousy, "the local yokel," was from Holy Cross, the Worcester, Massachusetts, college.

Auerbach did draft Share on the first round, claiming that his first obligation was to rebuild a losing franchise and the best way to start was with an All-American center. Then shortly before the start of the regular season, the Chicago team, which had drafted Cousy, folded and the league placed its players in a pool. The name of the Stags' three highest-priced players—Andy Phillip, Max Zaslofsky and Cousy—had been placed in a hat. Walter Brown, who had the third choice, pulled Cousy's name from the hat.

At this time, Auerbach made another significant move. Not one which was of great help in winning championships, but one much more important. He quietly helped break the color barrier in professional basketball by selecting Chuck Cooper, a forward from Duquesne, during the 1950 draft.

Slowly the Celtics became winners, and slowly Auerbach began building the nucleus for his championship run. Bill Sharman, the magnificent shooter, joined the club in 1952. In 1954, Frank Ramsey, the greatest sixth man in the game's history, reported to the Celtics. Then in 1956, Auerbach traded Macauley and Cliff Hagan to the St. Louis Hawks for the team's No. 1 draft choice. That choice was Bill Russell, the All-American center, who had just led the University of San Francisco to a couple of national collegiate titles. Auerbach added another player from that USF team. His name was K. C. Jones.

The Celtics won their first championship for Auerbach in 1956–57. But the next year, the St. Louis Hawks took the title away from Boston. In 1959 the Celtics came back to win, and they held the championship for eight straight seasons. Auerbach retired after that eighth championship.

During that time his teams had completely dominated the game. Their trademark was defense, a tough, clawing 48-minute defense that forced the opposition into errors. The cornerstone of the defense could be found in the middle, where Russell dominated the game. He blocked shots, he rebounded, and when he wasn't doing one of those two things, he simply intimidated the opposition, forcing them into bad shots and bad plays.

If the Celtics were the dominant team in the league

during these years, Auerbach was the dominant personality. It seemed everything he did was news. His fights with the league office seemed to be everyday occurrences. In many ways the cigar ceremony—which he started about 1956—typified Auerbach's defiant attitude. "When the league was pickin' on me for a thousand little things," Auerbach said, "I tried to think of something that would aggravate the higher-ups. I wasn't having much luck until one day when I lighted up a cigar during a game. Afterwards I got a little note saying, 'It doesn't look good for you to be smoking cigars on the bench.' So I told the guy who sent me the note that when the other coaches stopped smoking cigarettes, I'd put down my cigar." He never did put the cigar down.

Auerbach claims that the Boston management paid all but a "few cents" of the $17,000-plus in fines he accumulated over the years. A lot of fans wondered about the fines, wondered why Auerbach acted the way he did. They did not realize that Auerbach was, in addition to being a great coach, a first-rate psychologist.

"I tried to talk rules with the referees," Auerbach said, "because I wanted to get some consistency out there. Let every ref call a charge a charge. Some won't call walking because it doesn't affect play. But some will. It's the same with technical fouls. We had a rule there can be no talking by coaches to the refs on judgment calls. But some refs you can talk to and some you can't. If we have a rule, it should apply for all.

"I know some people criticized my arguments with the refs. But that's the way sport is. Who in basketball is tougher than Adolph Rupp or Ed Diddle? Does that make them bad coaches? A club must feel its coach is supporting them. If I think a ref blew one, it's my job to argue. It gives my team confidence. When I get clipped with a technical, it's right, but that doesn't mean I'm sorry. I'll be perfectly honest about it . . . there were times, few and far between, when I got up off that bench and raised a little dust not because the referees were doing a particularly bad job but because I had the feeling that my guys were half asleep out there and they needed some stirring up.

"Let's face it: You have to stay on the refs to make sure they're watching the other guys as well as yours. You have to keep asking them what about the other guy shoving, what about the other guy travelin', what about the other guy in the hole for 3 seconds, what about the other guy goaltending, what about the other guy charging, what about the other guy holding?

"If you don't too many of the calls are going against you, and you can't let that happen just because it's going to cost some money in fines, or because sportswriters are going to call you a ham who puts on temper tantrums just to intimidate the officials."

As the years passed, Auerbach's dynasty grew. He always had a nucleus to work with: first with Cousy and Sharman, then with Russell, Tom Heinsohn, Sam and K. C. Jones and Frank Ramsey and later with Russell, John Havlicek, Tom Sanders and still the Jones boys. Whenever Auerbach needed help he got it in trades or through the draft. There seemed to be no weaknesses, from the first man through the tenth or eleventh.

Chet Walker, a forward with the Syracuse Nationals and then the Philadelphia 76ers, once explained the frustration of playing against Boston. "I think," he said, "other teams have had personnel as good as Boston's, but on the other teams you're paid to be an all-around ballplayer. On the Celtics, you're paid to do one job. Take Satch Sanders. He's paid to play defense. He can concentrate on defense, and anything he gets on offense is a bonus. Sam Jones is paid to shoot. That's all he has to do."

Much of Auerbach's success can be traced to one of the man's fundamental principles: A team that survives the grueling NBA season is a team that is conditioned for it. During the first three days of the Celtics' pre-season training period, Auerbach's players concentrated on calisthenics and running drills. No one touched the basketball during the formal practices.

Auerbach had a theory about conditioning: "Maybe," he said, "my guys get back in the lineup a little quicker (after injuries) than most players . . . by being in such good condition to begin with. Some of my rookies don't play very much, but they know they better be in shape when I do need them or they are not going to stay around very long.

"One thing I've learned is never to allow a player to get himself in shape. They all have a tendency not to work hard enough and they always tell you they're ready before they actually are. You have to have strong legs to play basketball, which is why so much of our training revolves around the running game."

The nomadic life of the NBA was a lonely one for Auerbach. His wife, Dorothy, and his daughters, Nancy and Randy, remained in Washington during the winter months while Red was coaching the Celtics. Auerbach lived alone in Boston's Lenox Hotel, where his mantelpiece was covered with jars of pistachio and Indian nuts, paper-thin almonds and sunflower seeds.

His passion was Chinese food, and he was the league's leading expert on Chinese restaurants in NBA cities and points between. Maybe it was the schedule, with its 5 A.M. arrivals and its 7 A.M. departures, but Auerbach seldom took eggs and coffee for breakfast. He preferred a frankfurter and soft drink. His whole schedule was rather unusual. He was a coach who felt extreme pressure, but seldom showed it.

"I feel pressure like everybody else," he once said, "but on game days I do something about it. I actually create things to do—anything that will take my mind off the game. Fortunately, I've never had trouble sleeping."

For twenty years he lived the life of the wanderer. Then, at forty-eight, he retired and became executive vice-president and general manager of the Celtics. "I've had it," he said the day he announced his retirement. "It was tough enough doubling up last year as general manager and coach, and it's even tougher this year."

All that was left after winning the eighth straight title in the spring of 1966 was the team's annual break-up dinner. This one was a little special, a little more meaningful than all the others. This was Red Auerbach's last dinner as coach. Bill Russell would succeed him in September.

Russell was asked to speak. "I don't think I'm going to be another Red Auerbach," he told the diners and guest of honor. "Personally, I think you're the greatest basketball coach that ever lived. You know, over the years, I've heard a lot of coaches and writers say the only thing that made you a great coach was Bill Russell. I helped, but that's not what did it.

"Now, this is kind of embarrassing, but I'll go as far, Red, as to say this: I like you and I'll admit there aren't very many men that I like. But you I do. For a number of reasons. First of all, I've always been able to respect you. I don't think you're a genius, just an extraordinarily intelligent man. We'll be friends until one of us dies."

17

CLAIR BEE
The Innovator

The scholar, that was Clair Bee: assistant to the president of two colleges, a man who held five degrees, a writer, a television commentator, an accountant, farmer, outdoorsman. And one of the nation's most respected basketball coaches.

Energy and intellect propelled the man. So did an almost childlike love of sports, a love that would later wound him. Clair Bee was a gaunt, 150-pounder with deep-set eyes and a thin, bony face.

As a youngster in West Virginia he had suffered from tuberculosis. Ironically, misfortune became good fortune. His family physician urged the youngster to spend as much time out of doors as possible. "That prescription," Bee said, "helped to push me into sports."

His mother died from tuberculosis when he was six and young Clair spent part of his boyhood on his uncle's farm in Belleville, Kansas, part in Parkersburg and Grafton, West Virginia, and the rest at Massanutten Military Academy, Woodstock, Virginia.

By the time he was ten, basketball had become an

integral part of his life. He and his friends from the neighborhood in Grafton used to sneak into the gymnasium in the church and practice for hours. "After a while," Bee said, "the priests caught on, but they turned their heads the other way and let us keep playing. "They were happy to see us in church . . . even though it was only for basketball."

The priests didn't know it, but they were helping in the development of a man whose contributions to the game would be many before his career ended.

Clair Bee earned his fame at Long Island University, Brooklyn, N.Y. He also had coached at Waynesburg College, Waynesburg, Pennsylvania, and Rider College, Trenton, N.J. But LIU was his "home." Between 1931 and 1952, with the exception of two years when he was in the U.S. Navy, Bee's teams won 357 games and lost only 79. His teams won National Invitation Tournament championships in 1938–39, defeating Loyola of Chicago, 44–32, and in 1940–41, defeating Ohio State, 56–42. Two of his teams, the national-champion 1935–36 squad, and the 1938–39 squad, finished with unbeaten records, winning 25 and 23 games, respectively.

Over the years his teams ran off some of the game's longest winning streaks: 43, 38, 28, 26 and 20. The Blackbirds also managed a winning streak of 139 games at home in Brooklyn.

Bee originated basketball's "3-second rule" and the popular "one-three-one" zone defense. He also assisted in the development of the National Basketball Association's 24-second rule when he was coaching the Baltimore Bullets in the early 1950s.

Bee had another talent: he was an excellent writer specializing in technical books on basketball plus the extremely popular Chip Hilton sports series for youngsters. The Clair Bee Basketball Library, consisting of the *Science of Coaching, Fundamentals and Drills, Man-to-Man Defense and Attack* and *Zone Defense and Attack,* has been translated into Spanish, Portuguese and French.

He had one secret dream. He wanted to write a great novel. When he was a sophomore in high school in 1915, he wrote what may have been the first short story about basketball, titled, "Bud's Loyalty." Many years later Bee remarked, "I'm trying to write some other fiction, maybe a war story, completely divorced from sports. I write in trains, planes and on nights when I can't sleep—which means after every defeat . . . or after a victory when I expected to lose."

Bee's writing revealed a great deal about a complex man. The fictional Chip Hilton was the stereotype one expected from the brush of Norman Rockwell. Blond, blue-eyed, virtuous, intelligent, hardworking, a fine athlete with a strong sense of responsibility to his family, his church, his school, his friends and even his enemies, Chip Hilton belonged on Main Street, U.S.A.

Bee began writing the books while he was at LIU when that school was synonymous with high-powered athletics and basketball. LIU was one of the schools that packed Madison Square Garden night after night. It was an atmosphere completely alien to Chip Hilton, who might have, at some point in his career, led his team into Madison Square Garden, where it would have defeated LIU on one of Chip's last-second shots.

Clair Bee may have been an idealist, but he also was a realist who could fight and scratch and win in the toughest competition. He'd been a fighter dating back to the 1920s, when he applied for a job in a steel mill in Mansfield, Ohio.

If a person wanted a job in the mill—and Bee did since he had been married recently—it helped if the applicant played football. At 150 pounds, Bee seemed out of place in a league that included the Massillon Maroons and Canton Bulldogs. Bee made the mill team as a quarterback.

In one game against Massilon, the Mansfield ends were knocked out of the game with injuries. The Mansfield coach sent Bee into the lineup. On three successive plays, Bee leveled the well-known 200-pound back Fatty Fothergill.

Bee arrived at LIU in 1931 after a successful five-year stay at Rider College, where he coached the football and basketball teams and directed the accounting and business administration departments.

He immediately plunged into his numerous duties at LIU. He again headed the accounting and business administration departments at his new school, taught physical education classes and coached the baseball as well as basketball team.

Bee was a success as a basketball coach from the start; soon the Blackbirds challenged such New York City powerhouses as NYU, CCNY, Manhattan, Fordham and St. John's for the local headlines.

In 1934 a New York sportswriter, Ned Irish, realized there was a potentially huge market for college basketball, so he began promoting doubleheaders in Madison Square Garden, featuring New York City teams. LIU was one of the better attractions.

Between 1934 and 1936, LIU won 43 straight games before losing to Stanford, 45–31, in the Garden. Under Bee, LIU fielded national powerhouses until the basketball scandals rocked the collegiate sports world in 1951.

But until the sad ending, Bee was a popular and famous man whose teams attracted thousands of fans to the Garden and to its "home" gymnasium at Brooklyn College of Pharmacy, where from early in the 1937–

38 season until January 22, 1951, LIU won 139 straight games.

There were many highspots in Bee's coaching career including the two NIT championships. But there was one game, in December 1949, that Bee was extremely happy to win. It was against Oklahoma A&M, then one of the most powerful teams in basketball. Hank Iba, the master of the slow-down and defensive game, was coaching the Oklahomans.

Oklahoma A&M came into the Garden and Bee surprised everyone by doing to Iba what Hank had done to so many other teams. LIU played a deliberate, near-perfect game, taking only 28 shots. Each goal seemed to be worth 100 points, not 2, as LIU won, 38–31.

"What pointed up that game for me," Bee said, "was Iba's remark after he lost. Hank said, 'That little so-and-so held the ball on me!' That was my laugh of a lifetime. Imagine Hank complaining about anyone holding the ball on him!"

One of the characteristics of Bee-coached teams was a seven-man nucleus. He claimed he found it easier to practice with a group this size, continually switching and juggling men until the seven knew each other's moves perfectly.

"In a fast game," Bee said, "I believe teamwork is paramount. You cannot get precision teamwork with a large number of men; it has to be achieved with the same men practicing and working together as much as possible. I realized there is a grave danger in lack of depth—we pooped out that way one year—but if I can get seven good ones, I will go with them all the way, counting on their teamwork and conditioning to stay the season."

Bee often had his "seven good ones." Some of the finest players in college basketball played at LIU: Sherman White, Art Hillhouse, Bill King, Julie Bender, Dolly King, Irv Torgoff, Ossie Schechtman, Ben Kramer and Marius Russo, who later became a fine pitcher for the New York Yankees.

Clair Bee's life was full and rewarding until a cold February day in 1951 when the phone rang and the caller informed the proud little man that his world was about to dissolve. A number of basketball players from around the nation were involved in point-shaving scandals, including three LIU stars, White, Adolph Bigos and LeRoy Smith.

As an aftermath of the scandal, LIU canceled its future schedule and the school did not resume play until the 1957–58 season. Immediately after the scandal, Bee assumed an administrative post at the University. It was the darkest period of his life. "Clair's done," one of his assistant coaches said. "If he lives through this and lives to see another basketball season, I'll be surprised."

As the days and then the months passed and the wounds began to close, Bee spoke about what had happened. He accepted the blame for part of it.

Addressing a banquet in Newport News, Virginia, that same year, Bee told the assembled guests, many of whom were coaches, "We—you and I—have flunked. We have not done the job that was expected of us in training the young people. I am not bitter. I am hurt, hurt desperately. When I was told that three of my boys had sold themselves it was a deep bereavement. I am not ashamed to say that I wept. . . . It was then that something died within me."

Almost a year later, Bee looked back on the scandal and said, "Public confidence in college basketball is shattered, and the fault is partly mine. I was a 'win-em-all' coach who, by resorting to established practices, helped to create the emotional climate that led to the worst scandal in the history of sports.

"I—every coach under the pressure of big-time sport —was so absorbed in the victory grail that I lost sight of the educational purposes of athletics. They say the loudest psalm singer is a reformed sinner. . . . I still believe competitive sports have a high educational value when handled properly."

The great irony in Bee's case was his fictional hero, Chip Hilton, the perfect boy and athlete who never committed a wrong. "Yes," Bee said, "Chip is the type of boy I would have wanted to coach."

All during the glory years at LIU, Bee must have been a tortured person, hoping for one thing, one way of life, Chip Hilton's way of life, while in reality living a completely different life.

It was a life full of pressure. In the spring of 1964, in Monticello, N.Y., where he had a boys camp, Bee admitted that he led something of a double life. "It is a shame that college coaches are forced to fight to get players to come to their schools, but that's where success lies," he said. "A coach makes his living by recruiting, and I was as good a recruiter as anyone else.

"I guess I was too concerned with my own doings. Each coach says it couldn't happen to him. I refused to believe it when it happened, because I never suspected a player. You know, in my opinion, a coach is like a father. He is the last to recognize the weaknesses of his son, and if he recognizes imperfections he can't believe it because his hopes for the youngster are so high. When it happened, I tried to black it out of my mind. I wanted to wrap myself up in something else."

For a while it was professional coaching, then teaching again at New York Military Academy, and then running his camp and farm. All that time he continued to write his Chip Hilton novels and they continued to sell well among sports-minded youngsters.

"The books are a real source of satisfaction," he said, "because I get letters every day from boys telling me how much they enjoyed and learned from them."

Clair Bee chose the quiet life, the country life of upstate New York. It was a life far-removed from the screaming crowds of Madison Square Garden, the basketball polls and the pressures of recruiting.

"I had my fill," he said. "I wouldn't want to go through all those headaches again. Not at my age. I'm just content with things as they are at school, my farm and the writing."

The ultimate tribute to Clair Bee came after the scandals. It came in the form of numerous invitations from his fellow coaches to address their clinics and banquets and talk about basketball, Clair Bee's basketball. Winning basketball.

DIRECTORY
of Hall of Fame Members

The following persons and teams have been elected to the Hall of Fame:

DR. FORREST CLARE (PHOG) ALLEN

Elected as contributor 1959...Birth: Jamesport, Mo., Nov. 18, 1885...Basketball coach at Baker University, Haskell Indian Institute, Central Teachers College, Warrensburg, Mo., and University of Kansas...Kansas national champions 1922–23, 1923-24, 1951–52... Teams won 771 games...Co-founder of National Association of Basketball Coaches, 1927...Instrumental in placing basketball on Olympic program...NABC president, 1927–29...Director of Athletics, University of Kansas, 1919–38...Director of Physical Education Department, University of Kansas, 1923–42...Graduate, University of Kansas...I.C.C. College of Osteopathy and Surgery, Kansas City.

ARNOLD (RED) AUERBACH

Elected as coach 1968...Birth: Brooklyn, N.Y., Sept. 20, 1917...Winningest coach of all time, 1,037–548, with Washington, Tri-Cities and Boston of the BAA and NBA...Under Auerbach Celtics formed one of basketball's great dynasties...Won nine divisional titles, eight straight world titles...Coached eleven straight East teams in NBA All-Star game...NBA Coach of the Year 1965...His teams dominated the pro game between 1956 and 1966...Washington, D.C., Touchdown Club Coach of the Decade...Coached some of the game's greats: Bob Cousy, Bill Russell, Bill Sharman, Ed Macauley, Sam Jones, K.C. Jones, many more.

JOHN BECKMAN

Elected as player 1973...Birth: New York, N.Y., Oct. 22, 1895...Died: June 22, 1968...Known in the 1920s and part of the '30s as the "Babe Ruth of Basketball" for his play with the Original Celtics...Captained the Celtics...Played in a number of professional leagues and with a number of teams beginning in 1910 with St. Gabriels of New York...Pro clubs included Kingston, N.Y., Paterson, N.J., Nanticoke, Pa., Philadelphia and Baltimore in addition to the Celtics...He was one of the main reasons the Celtics were elected to the Hall of Fame as a team.

CLAIR FRANCIS BEE

Elected as coach 1967...Birth: Grafton, W. Va., March 2, 1900...Coached Mansfield, Ohio, High School, Rider College, Long Island University, Baltimore Bullets, New York Military Academy...Originated basketball's 3-second rule, one-three-one zone defense...Assisted in development of NBA 24-second rule...Coached two National Invitation Tournament champions at LIU... Prolific author of children's fiction and technical basketball books...West Virginia Hall of Fame...Madison

Square Garden Hall of Fame...Degrees: B.A. Waynesburg College...M.C.S. Rider College...M.A. Rutgers University.

ERNEST BLOOD

Elected as coach 1960...Birth: Manchester, N.H., Oct. 4, 1872...Died: Feb. 5, 1955...Coached YMCA teams in Somerville, Mass., Rutland, Vt., Nashua, N.H., Brooklyn, N.Y., 1895–1906...Potsdam N.Y., High School, Clarkson University coach 1906–15...Coached Passaic, N.J., High School, 1915–24...St. Benedict's Prep, 1924–49...U.S. Military Academy, West Point, 1925–26...Passaic High School had 200–1 record under his coaching...Potsdam, 72–2...St. Benedict's, 421–128...Passaic seven times high school champion...St. Benedict's five times prep school champs...West Point record, 16–2...Clarkson record 40–5.

BERNHARD BORGMANN

Elected as player 1961...Birth: Haledon, N.J., Nov. 21, 1899...Nickname "Benny"...Member of Original Celtics...Also played for Paterson Crescents, Paterson Legionnaires, Kingston Colonels, Fort Wayne Hoosiers (1918–42)...Participated in 2,500 professional games ...High scorer in every league in which he competed... Coached at St. Michael's College and Muhlenberg College...Professional coach with Syracuse and Paterson... Big-league baseball scout.

WALTER BROWN

Elected as contributor 1965...Birth: Hopkinton, Mass., Feb. 10, 1905...Died Sept. 7, 1964...Founded National Basketball Association June 6, 1946...Organized Boston

Celtics...Chairman, Hall of Fame Board of Directors, 1961–64...President Boston Garden, 1937–64...President Bruins Hockey Club...Promoted college basketball doubleheaders in Boston Garden...Underwrote $5,000 Naismith commemorative stamp.

JOHN BUNN

Elected as contributor 1964...Birth: Wellston, Ohio, Sept. 26, 1898...Coach at Stanford, Springfield College and Colorado State (Greeley)...Editor of *Basketball Guide* and Official Rules Interpreter 1959–67...Chairman, Basketball Hall of Fame Committee, National Association of Basketball Coaches 1949–64...NABC president 1949–50...Author of numerous basketball books...Coached All-American Hank Luisetti at Stanford...Won Pacific Coast Conference titles 1936, 1937 and 1938.

HOWARD GOODSELL CANN

Elected as coach 1967...Birth: Oct. 11, 1895, Bridgeport, Conn....All-American forward 1920 for NYU's AAU champions...Coach at NYU 1922–58, 409–232 ...Helms Hall of Fame...Member U.S. Olympic team 1920...Coach NYU football team 1932–33...IC4A shotput champion while student at NYU...Tackle and fullback on football team...B.S. Industrial Engineering, NYU.

DR. HENRY CLIFFORD CARLSON

Elected as coach 1959...Birth: Murray City, Ohio, July 4, 1894...Died: Nov. 1, 1964...Coached University of Pittsburgh 1922–53...Developed the "figure-8" offense...1927–28 team, 21–0...Overall record, 370–246...1927–28 and 1929–30 teams considered national champions...First to take Eastern team to west coast in 1931–32...President National Association Basketball Coaches 1937...Received medical degree from University of Pittsburgh, practiced medicine and directed Mens Student Health Department at Pitt, 1932–64.

BEN CARNEVALE

Elected as coach 1969...Birth: Raritan, N.J., Oct. 30, 1915...Coached Cranford, N.J., High School to 75 wins, 1939–42...Then coached at North Carolina U., and had 51 wins between 1944 and '46...From there he moved to U.S. Naval Academy where his teams won 257 games in 20 years...Collegiate Coach of the Year 1947...President, National Association Basketball Coaches, 1966...Played for NYU.

BOB COUSY

Elected as player 1970...Birth: New York City, Aug. 9, 1928...All-American at Holy Cross College 1948, 1949, 1950... Joined Boston Celtics 1950...Led them to five straight titles, 1959–63...Played on six NBA championship teams in seven years, 1956–63...All-NBA first team 10 years in row...MVP in 1957...All-Star game MVP 1954, 1957...Had 6,959 assists...Scored 16,960 points...Later coached Boston College, Cincinnati Royals.

BOB DAVIES

Elected as player 1969...Birth: Harrisburg, Pa., Jan. 15, 1920...Two-time All-American at Seton Hall...Led team to 43 straight wins...MVP in 1942 College All-Star game...Joined Rochester Royals in 1945 for a 10-year pro career...All-league 7 times...MVP 1947...Led

Royals to World Titles in 1946, '47 and '51...Scored 7, 771 points as a tricky, crowd-pleasing guard.

EVERETT DEAN

Elected as coach 1966...Birth: Livonia, Ind., March 18, 1898...All Western Conference center 1921, University of Indiana...Coached Carleton College 1921–24...University of Indiana 1924–38...Stanford University 1938–55...Indiana Hall of Fame... Indiana coaching, 162–93...Member Attorney General's National Sports Committee 1947–48...Vice-president, treasurer, National Association Basketball Coaches.

FORREST DE BERNARDI

Elected as player 1961...Birth: Nevada, Mo., Feb. 3, 1899...Died: April 29, 1970...One of finest players to come out of amateur ranks...Played for Kansas City Athletic, Hillyard Chemical Co. and Cook Paint Co. teams 1920–29...AAU All-American 1921, 1922, 1923...Played in AAU finals 1923 and 1925, and played on AAU champions 1926 and 1927 with Hillyard...Graduate, Westminster College, Fulton, Mo.

HENRY (DUTCH) DEHNERT

Elected as player 1968...Birth: New York City, April 5, 1898...Without high school or college training, had memorable pro career in Eastern professional leagues before joining Original Celtics in 1920...Credited with developing pivot play...Became famous for its execution and success...Celtics and Cleveland Rosenblums won 1,900 games when he was in lineup...Coached Detroit Eagles to pro titles in 1940 and 1941...Also coached Sheboygan, Wis., team.

ED DIDDLE

Elected as coach 1971...Birth: Gradyville, Ky., March 12, 1895...Death: Jan. 2, 1970...Graduate of Centre College 1920...Started at Western Kentucky in 1922 and for the next 42 years he had one of the nation's most consistent teams...Fast-breaking Hilltoppers won or shared in 32 conference titles, participated in 3 NCAA, 8 NIT tournaments...Had 759 wins.

ROBERT DOUGLAS

Elected as contributor 1971...Birth: St. Kitts, B.W.I., Nov. 4, 1884...Came to America at age four...First black elected to Hall of Fame...Organized the famed New York Rennaissance Five in 1922...Played mostly touring games...In 22 years the team won 2,318, including 88 straight in 1933...Won 128 in 1934...1939 World Pro Champions...Bob coached Rens throughout their golden era.

BRUCE DRAKE

Elected as coach 1973...Birth: Gentry, Tex., Dec. 5, 1905...Though much of his fame came through coaching, he also made the Helms All-America team in 1929 when he was the captain at the University of Oklahoma...Later became head coach at Oklahoma for 17 seasons and invented the "Drake Shuffle"...His teams won 200 games and captured or tied for the conference championship six times...Oklahoma lost the national championship game to Holy Cross in 1947...A former president of the National Collegiate Coaches' Association...Assistant coach of 1956 U.S. Olympic team.

PAUL ENDACOTT

Elected as player 1971...Birth: Lawrence, Kan., July 13, 1902...Played at University of Kansas...Phog Allen called him "the greatest player I ever coached"...Led Jayhawks to mythical national title 1923...Helms Foundation Player of Year 1923...His abilities withstood the passing of the years and in 1969 Dr. Allen selected him for the national all-time college team.

HAROLD (BUD) FOSTER

Elected as player 1964...Birth: Newton, Kan., May 30, 1906...All-American for University of Wisconsin 1930 ...Center and forward...All Western Conference 1929 and 1930...Captain 1930 Wisconsin team...During his three varsity years Wisconsin lost only 7 games...Later coached at Wisconsin...Pro career with Duffy Florals of Chicago.

MARTY FRIEDMAN

Elected as player 1971...Birth: New York City, July 12, 1889...Played for University Settlement House Metropolitan A.A.U. champs 1906–08...Turned pro in 1909 with New York Roosevelts...Considered one of first defensive stars of early pro leagues in East... Finished career as captain and coach of Cleveland Rosenblums 1923–27...Only 5-8, but helped win many championships.

AMORY (SLATS) GILL

Elected as coach 1967...Birth: Salem, Ore., May 1, 1901...Died: April 5, 1966...All-American guard Oregon State University 1924...Later head coach Oregon State, beginning 1924...Coached 36 years, compiling 599–392 record...Five Pacific Coast Conference champions...Past president National Association Basketball Coaches...Helms Foundation Hall of Fame... Tournament director NCAA championships, 1965.

EDDIE GOTTLIEB

Elected as contributor 1971...Birth: Kiev, Russia, Sept. 15, 1898...One of early organizers of pro game ...Coached the famed Philadelphia SPHAS, beginning 1918...They peaked in 1925–26 when defeated Original Celtics and Original Rens...Later dominated Eastern and American Basketball Leagues...Eddie helped organize the Basketball Association of America in 1946... His Philadelphia Warriors won first BAA title...BAA later became NBA and Warriors joined it...Eddie coached until 1955–56.

ROBERT (ACE) GRUENIG

Elected as player 1963...Birth: Chicago, Ill., March 12, 1913...Died: Aug. 11, 1958...Outstanding AAU player with Rosenberg-Arvey of Chicago, Denver Safeways, Denver Nuggets, Denver American Legion, Denver Ambrose and Murphy-Mahoney, 1933–48...First-team AAU All-American ten times...One of game's early big men at 6-8, 220.

DR. LUTHER GULICK

Elected as contributor 1959...Birth: Honolulu, Hawaii, Dec. 4, 1865...Died: Aug. 13, 1918...Met Dr. James Naismith while teaching at Springfield College, helped in development of the game...Profound influence on

Naismith as director of physical education at Springfield...Later became director of physical education for New York Public School system...Set up New York's famous Public Schools Athletic League...One of the game's first boosters...Former chairman AAU basketball committee.

VICTOR HANSON

Elected as player 1960...Birth: Watertown, N.Y., July 30, 1903...Great all-around athlete at Syracuse University...Earned nine varsity letters...Basketball All-American 1925, 1926 and 1927...Player of the Year, Helms Athletic Foundation 1927...Led 1925–26 team to national championship with 19–1 record...Syracuse 48–7 during his career...Scored 25 of Syracuse's 30 points in victory over Pennsylvania in 1926...All-time All-American as selected by Grantland Rice...Played professionally with Cleveland Rosenblums...Former head football coach at Syracuse...Signed with New York Yankees in baseball.

GEORGE HEPBRON

Elected as referee 1960...Birth: Still Pond, Md., Aug. 27, 1863...Died: April 30, 1946...First basketball official in New York area...Organized Brooklyn YMCA league...Editor of AAU basketball guide 1901–14... Member AAU rules committee, 1896–1915...Member and secretary, joint rules committee 1915–36... Traveled extensively encouraging game and referees... In 1904 wrote first book on how to play the game.

EDWARD J. HICKOX

Elected as contributor 1959...Birth: Cleveland, Ohio, April 10, 1878...Died: Jan. 28, 1966...Coached

Springfield College basketball team for sixteen years and American International College for one season... First executive secretary of Hall of Fame...President National Association of Basketball Coaches 1944–46 ...Introduced basketball at Lycoming College in 1907 ...Eaton, Colo., high school team won 1911 high school championship of Colorado, Wyoming and Northern New Mexico...His 1912 high school team defeated five college teams, incluidng Rocky Mt. champion, Colorado School of Mines.

PAUL (TONY) HINKLE

Elected as contributor 1965...Birth: Logansport, Ind., Dec. 19, 1899...Began coaching basketball at Butler University, Indianapolis 1924...534–366 through 39 seasons...Member, NCAA rules committee 1953–54; chairman, 1955–56...President National Association Basketball Coaches 1954–55...All Western Conference for University of Chicago...Helms All-American 1920 ...Coached Butler to national championship in 1929... During World War II coached Great Lakes team to 98 victories...Football and baseball coach at Butler...Also director of athletics...Professor and director of Physical Education department.

HOWARD HOBSON

Elected as coach 1965...Birth: Portland, Ore., July 4, 1903...Coach at Kelso, Wash., High School, Benson, Ore., High School, Southern Oregon College, University of Oregon, Yale University 1927–53...Had 495–291 record...1939 Oregon team won first NCAA tournament...Oregon teams were among first from West to travel East for intersectional games...Conducted numerous basketball clinics in U.S. and fifteen foreign countries...President, National Association Basketball Coaches 1947...Served twelve years on U.S. Olympic Basketball Committee...Record at Oregon, 211–124.

NAT HOLMAN

Elected as player 1964...Birth: New York City, Oct. 18, 1896...Member and star player Original Celtics ...Coach CCNY 38 years...Coached National Collegiate Champion and National Invitation Tournament champion 1950...President National Association Basketball Coaches 1941...*Sport* magazine Coach of the Year 1950...Professor, Department Physical Education CCNY...Graduate Savage School of Physical Education.

GEORGE HOYT

Elected as referee 1961...Birth: South Boston, Mass., Aug. 9, 1883...Died: Nov. 11, 1962...First listed in directory of registered officials 1911...One of best-known referees in New England...Organized first official referees' board in eastern Massachusetts...One of the pioneers in officiating the game and introducing the job of the referee to others.

CHARLES (CHUCK) HYATT

Elected as player 1959...Birth: Syracuse, N.Y., Feb. 28, 1908...All-American forward, University of Pittsburgh 1929–30...Led Pitt to first national title in 1927–28, scoring 266 points...Scored 314 points in 1929–30 ...Hit an even 300 as a junior...Played in only six losing games in three years...One of great scorers of his time ...Later an AAU All-American for nine years.

HENRY (HANK) IBA

Elected as coach 1968...Birth: Easton, Mo., Aug. 6, 1904...Coaching success from beginning at Classen, Okla., High School...Maryville, Mo., Teachers runner-up for national title in 1932...Moved to Oklahoma A&M, now Oklahoma State, where he won fourteen conference titles...In 1945 and 1946 his teams won consecutive national collegiate titles...Only coach to guide two U.S. Olympic teams, 1964 and 1968, to gold medals...President National Association Basketball Coaches 1968.

EDWARD SIMMONS (NED) IRISH

Elected as contributor 1964...Birth: Lake George, N.Y., May 6, 1905...Introduced the basketball double-header to Madison Square Garden on large-scale basis in 1934...That move credited with making basketball a major sport...New York and the Garden became mecca of basketball as the game, because of Irish, went intersectional...Founded New York Knickerbockers 1946.

R. WILLIAM JONES

Elected as contributor 1964...Birth: Rome, Italy, Oct. 5, 1906...Co-founder International Basketball Federation 1932...Introduced basketball in Olympics 1936... Executive Secretary, F.I.B.A., since 1932...Organized numerous international tourments...Director, UNESCO Youth Institute, Munich, Germany.

ALVIN (DOGGIE) JULIAN

Elected as coach 1967...Birth: Reading, Pa., April 5, 1901...Died: July 28, 1967...The coach who brought about a renaissance of basketball in Boston and Worcester, Mass....Coached at Muhlenberg College, Allentown, Pa., before coming to Holy Cross 1945–46...1947 Holy Cross team won NCAA title...Later coached at Dartmouth College...Coached Bob Cousy, Joe Mullaney, George Kaftan, Frank Oftring and Bob Curran at Holy Cross...65–10 record in three years there...More than 400 lifetime victories...His teams participated in five NCAA tournaments and two National Invitation Tournaments...1966 president of Coaches Association.

FRANK KEANEY

Elected as coach 1960...Birth: Boston, Mass., June 5, 1886...Died: Oct. 10, 1967...Coach Putnam, Conn., High School; Woonsocket R.I., High School; Everett, Mass., High School...University of Rhode Island 1920–48...Record at Rhode Island 401-124...Coached four NIT entrants...Athletic Director University of Rhode Island...Graduate Bates College 1911...Set college record in baseball with .410 average and 38 stolen bases.

MATTHEW (PAT) KENNEDY

Elected as referee 1959...Birth: Hoboken, N.J., Jan. 28, 1908...Died: June 16, 1957...Most famous referee in game's history...High school, college and professional official 1928–46...Supervisors of officials in NBA 1946–50...Toured with Harlem Globetrotters from 1950 through 1957...Often worked ten games a week, 125 per season...A gate attraction in his own right because of his colorful mannerisms on the court.

GEORGE KEOGAN

Elected as coach 1961...Birth: Minnesota Lakes, Minn., March 8, 1890...Died: Feb. 17, 1943...Successful coach at St. Louis University, Valparaiso University, Notre Dame...Record at Notre Dame 1923–43, 327–96...Created "shifting man-to-man" defense...From 1935 through 1937 season, Fighting Irish won 42 lost only 5 and were one of nation's best teams.

BOB KURLAND

Elected as player 1961...Birth: St. Louis, Mo., Dec. 23, 1924...Led Oklahoma A&M to successive national collegiate titles in 1945–46...Played for 1948 and 1952 U.S. Olympic teams...Most Valuable Player NCAA tournament 1945, 1946...Consensus All-American, 1944–46...National scoring champion 1946 ...AAU standout with Phillips Oilers...One of first really talented big men at 7 foot...Made AAU All-American team 1947–52.

WARD (PIGGY) LAMBERT

Elected as coach 1960...Birth: Deadwood, S.D., May 28, 1888...Died: Jan. 20, 1958...Head coach Purdue University 1916–46...His Purdue teams won or shared eleven Western Conference Big Ten championships...Overall record, 371–152...Pioneered fast-break game...Coached many All-Americans including Hall of Famer John Wooden...Commissioner National Professional Basketball League 1946–49.

JOE LAPCHICK

Elected as player 1966...Birth: Yonkers, N.Y., April 12, 1900....Died: August 10, 1970...Gained his fame as first legitimate "star" center in game when he played for Original Celtics...Also played briefly with Cleveland Rosenblums...Played pro ball from 1917 to 1936... Later coached at St. John's University, where his teams won four National Invitation Tournament titles...Also coached New York Knickerbockers of NBA...Twice national college Coach of Year.

KEN LOEFFLER

Elected as coach 1964...Birth: Beaver Falls, Pa., April 14, 1902...Coached at Geneva College 1928–34; Yale 1934–42; St. Louis Bombers professional team 1946–49; LaSalle College 1949–55; Texas A&M 1955–57... Coached 1954 LaSalle team to national championship ...Had his greatest years with Explorers, 145–27... Coached Tom Gola, considered by many to be the greatest collegiate player of all time...Professor of law... Also worked as a newspaper columnist in Pittsburgh 1924–29.

DUTCH LONBORG

Elected as coach 1973...Birth: Gardner, Ill., March 16, 1898...Spent 29 years coaching college basketball teams...Started with McPherson College, moved to Washburn University and then spent 23 seasons at Northwestern...In 1925, his Washburn team won the AAU championship, the last time a college was able to win the crown...In 1931, he coached Northwestern to its first Big Ten championship...Served as president of the coaches' association in 1935 and as manager of the U.S. Olympic team in 1960.

ANGELO (HANK) LUISETTI

Elected as player 1959...Birth: San Francisco, Calif., June 16, 1916...Revolutionized the game with one-hand shot...Led Stanford to three consecutive Pacific Coast titles 1936–38...Three-time All-American...Recognized as greatest player in coast history...Scored 1,596 points in four-year career...Scored 50 points against Duquesne in his senior year.

ED (EASY ED) MACAULEY

Elected as player 1960...Birth: St. Louis, Mo., March 22, 1928...Youngest person elected to Hall of Fame... Two-time All-American St. Louis University...Player of the Year 1947, 1948...Most Valuable Player National Invitation Tournament 1948...Led nation in field-goal percentage with .524 average in 1946–47...Led St. Louis to NIT title 1948; Sugar Bowl title following sea-son...Played professionally with St. Louis, Boston... Played in eight NBA All-Star games...Career high of 46 vs. George Mikan and Minneapolis Lakers, March 6, 1953...Coached St. Louis Hawks to Western Division titles 1958–60.

BRANCH McCRACKEN

Elected as player 1960...Birth: Monrovia, Ind., June 9, 1908...Died: June 4, 1970...Played three years at Indiana University under Everett Dean...Led team in scoring all three years...In senior year set Western Con-ference record of 147 points...Consensus All-American 1929–30...Scored 525 career points...That was 32 per-cent of points scored by Indiana during the three-year period...Later coached at Indiana 1938–65...Teams won 275, lost 119...Won national titles in 1940 and 1953...Coach of the Year 1940, 1953.

JUMPIN' JACK McCRACKEN

Elected as player 1962...Birth: Chickasha, Okla., June 11, 1911...Died: Jan. 5, 1958...Played high school and college basketball for Henry Iba...All-American at Northwest Missouri Teachers College...Considered by Iba one of finest players he coached...Consistently named to AAU All-American teams between 1932 and 1942, when he played for Denver teams and Phillips 66ers.

WALTER MEANWELL

Elected as coach 1959...Birth: Leeds, England, Jan. 26, 1884...Died: Dec. 2, 1953...Coached at University of Wisconsin...University of Missouri...Record 290–101...Eleven conference championships...Helms Hall of Fame; Wisconsin Hall of Fame...Developed valve for laceless basketball...Also developed the basketball shoe that bore his name...One of pioneers in giving clinics...Traveled all over United States...Author on basketball and conditioning.

GEORGE MIKAN

Elected as player 1960...Birth: Joliet, Ill., June 18, 1924...Three-time All-American center at DePaul... Scored 1,870 points in four years...53 in NIT game against Rhode Island, 1945...Player of the year 1944–45 and 1945–46...Associated Press' player of the half century...One of all-time pro greats with Minneapolis Lakers...First Commissioner of the American Basketball Association, 1967.

WILLIAM MOKRAY

Elected as contributor 1965...Birth: Passaic, N.J., June 6, 1907...Editor *Official NBA Guide*...Author *Basketball Encyclopedia* 1963...Wrote history of basketball for *Encyclopedia Brittanica* 1957...First chairman, Hall of Fame Honors Committee 1959–64...Scout and promotion director, Boston Celtics...Basketball director Boston Garden...Author of basketball books and articles.

RALPH MORGAN

Elected as contributor 1959...Birth: Philadelphia, Pa., Mar. 9, 1884...Died: Jan. 5, 1965...Founded collegiate basketball rules committee 1905...Secretary-Treasurer, Eastern Intercollegiate Basketball League...Founded Eastern Collegiate Basketball League, now Ivy League, in 1910.

FRANK (POP) MORGENWECK

Elected as contributor 1962...Birth: Egg Harbor, N.J., July 15, 1875...Died: Dec. 8, 1941...Spent 32 years managing, financing and promoting early professional games...Coached Kingston, N.Y., to New York State and world's pro championship 1922–23...Coached Rochester Centrals to American League title 1929–30 ...Discovered Original Celtic stars Benny Borgmann and Johnny Beckman...Coached Chicago Bruins for George Halas.

CHARLES (STRETCH) MURPHY

Elected as player 1960...Birth: Marion, Ind., April 10, 1907...Purdue University All-American at 6-9 under Ward Lambert...Played from 1926 through 1930...Set

Western Conference record of 143 points in 1929...
Captained 1930 conference championship team...
Teamed with Johnny Wooden in 1930...Helms Foundation All-American three years.

DR. JAMES NAISMITH

Elected as contributor 1959...Birth: Almonte, Ontario, Nov. 6, 1861...Died: Nov. 28, 1939...Invented basketball at Springfield College, December 1891, then promoted the game all over country...M.A. Physical Education 1910...Studied for ministry at Presbyterian College, Montreal...Director of Physical Education McGill University 1887...Instructor YMCA Training School, Springfield, Mass....Ordained Presbyterian Minister 1915...Received medical degree Gross Medical School 1898...Physical Education Denver YMCA 1895 ...Head of Physical Education Department, University of Kansas 1898–1925...Retired from teaching 1937... Little-known fact is that while at Springfield he tested and wore first football helmet.

JOHN J. O'BRIEN, SR.

Elected as contributor 1961...Birth: Brooklyn, N.Y., Nov. 4, 1888...Died: Dec. 9, 1967...Organized Metropolitan Basketball League 1921...President, American Basketball League, 25 years...Leading professional and college official for twenty years...Assisted in organizing Interstate Pro Basketball League in 1914...Served as its president 1915–17...Officiated many early pro games around New York, city and state.

HAROLD G. OLSEN

Elected as contributor 1959...Birth: Rice Lake, Wis., May 12, 1895...Died: Oct. 29, 1953...Basketball coach at Ohio State 1922–46...Won conference titles 1925, 1939, 1944 and 1946...Past president, coaches association...Former chairman NCAA rules committee, NCAA tournament committee...Member of 1948 Olympic basketball committee...Helped introduce the 10-second rule...Coached Chicago Stags pro team 1946–49.

H.O. (PAT) PAGE

Elected as player 1962...Birth: Chicago, Ill., March 20, 1887...Died: Nov. 23, 1965...Player of the year 1910 while at Chicago U....Led team to national title in 1908, undefeated season in 1909...Western Conference titles in 1907, 1909, 1910...Played guard...Effective left-handed shooter...Later basketball coach at Chicago U. 1911–20...Also coached at Butler, 1930-33.

BOB PETTIT

Elected as player 1970...Birth: Dec. 12, 1932, Baton Rouge, La....All-American at LSU 1952–54...NBA Rookie of Year, 1954–55...Played forward...All-league first team 10 straight years for Milwaukee and St. Louis Hawks...NBA MVP 1956, '59...All-Star game MVP four times...Retired in 1965 as highest scorer in NBA history with 20,880 points...Third best rebounder in league history.

ANDY PHILLIP

Elected as player 1961...Birth: Granite City, Ill., March 7, 1922...Leader of famed "Whiz Kids" team at University of Illinois...Two-time All-American... Elected to Associated Press' all-time All-American team...Set Western Conference records for most points season (255), most field goals (16) and most points (40) in a single game...Played 1941–42, 1942–43, then entered service and returned for 1946–47 season ...Later played pro ball with Chicago Stags, Philadelphia Warriors, Fort Wayne Pistons and Boston Celtics.

HENRY PORTER

Elected as contributor 1960...Birth: Oct. 2, 1891...As director of the National Federation of State High School Athletic Associations he helped organize the National Basketball Committee of U.S. and Canada...First representative of high schools on NABC, member thirty years...Codified rules of basketball with Oswald Tower ...Pioneered invention and adoption of molded ball and use of films for rules study...Author of basketball books...His player handbook and other books sold 10 million copies.

ERNEST QUIGLEY

Elected as referee 1961...Birth: New Castle, N.B., Canada, March 22, 1880...Died: Dec. 10, 1968...College and AAU basketball official for forty years 1904–44...Supervisor, NCAA tournament officials 1940–42 ...Also a baseball umpire in National League...Umpired at many World Series...Played basketball under Dr. James Naismith at Kansas.

WILLIAM REID

Elected as contributor 1963...Birth: Detroit, Mich., Sept. 26, 1893...Died: Oct. 30, 1955...Basketball coach and director of athletics Colgate University...

Coached ten years, director 36 years...President Eastern Collegiate Athletic Conference 1944–45...Vice-president National Collegiate Athletic Association 1942-46... Record as coach at Colgate, 151–56...Also famous for his play during military days with American Expeditionary Force team which won AEF title in 1919... Averaged 17.3 points per game in AEF ball, unheard of in that era.

ELMER RIPLEY

Elected as player 1973...Birth: Staten Island, N.Y., July 21, 1891...A 20-year career with a number of championship teams, including the Original Celtics... His pro career started with the Carbondale, Pa., team ...Also played for Scranton, the Original Celtics, Fort Wayne K. of C., Brooklyn and Cleveland...Later turned to coaching at Georgetown, Yale, Columbia, Notre Dame, Army and Regis...Conducted many clinics and toured Israel for the U.S. Dept. of State...Coached the 1960 Canadian Olympic team...Had a three-year stint as coach of the Harlem Globetrotters.

JOHN ROOSMA

Elected as player 1961...Birth: Passaic, N.J., Sept. 3, 1900...Led West Point through unbeaten season (31 games) in 1922–23...Received All-American notice... On all-time New Jersey team...One of Ernest Blood's all-time favorites at Passaic High School...Outstanding athlete class of 1926, West Point...Later coached and played for many military teams both in the United States and overseas...Also refereed major-college games.

ADOLPH RUPP

Elected as coach 1968...Birth: Halstead, Kan., Sept. 2, 1901...Played for Phog Allen at University of Kansas ...Member of 1923 national-championship team...Allen's protégé became most successful college coach in history, winning his 800th game during the 1968–69 season at University of Kentucky, where he began coaching in 1930...Kentucky teams winners of 24 Southeastern Conference titles, four NCAA titles, one NIT championship...Co-coach 1948 U.S. Olympic team...Four times Coach of the Year...Eleven overseas clinics.

JOHN (HONEY) RUSSELL

Elected as player 1964..Birth: Brooklyn, N.Y., May 31, 1903...Played in more than 3,200 professional basketball games with Brooklyn Visitations, Cleveland Rosenblums, Chicago Bruins, Rochester Centrals ...Also coached Chicago franchise...One of best scoring guards in early days of pro game...Once held early pro scoring record of 22 points in one game...Successful coach at Seton Hall University in New Jersey after retiring as player...Big-league baseball scout.

LEONARD SACHS

Elected as coach 1961...Birth: Chicago, Ill., Aug. 7, 1897...Died: Oct. 27, 1942...Had 224–129 record at Loyola of Chicago from 1924–42...Noted for his defensive strategy...His 1927–28, 1928–29 teams won 32 straight games...1938–39 team lost only 1 game, to LIU in NIT finals...Member of Illinois Athletic Club team that won AAU title in 1918.

ABE SAPERSTEIN

Elected 1970 as contributor...Birth: London, England, July 4, 1902...Death: March 15, 1966...Settled in Chicago...Formed famed touring comedy team called Harlem Globetrotters...Played before 55 million fans in 87 countries, including 75,000 in Berlin...Team won World Pro title in 1940...Won International Cup in 1943, '44...Credited with making basketball a truly international game.

ARTHUR SCHABINGER

Elected as contributor 1961...Birth: Sabetha, Kan., Aug. 6, 1889...Died: October 13, 1972...Basketball coach at Creighton University for thirteen years (169–67), Ottawa University (Kan.), Emporia Teachers College...Co-founder of National Association Basketball Coaches...Member of rules committee 1935–36 ...Founder and director of officials' sport-film service ...NABC president 1931–32...Early advocate of intersectional scheduling...Basketball official in Midwest... Conducted tryouts for first U.S. Olympic team.

DOLPH SCHAYES

Elected as player 1973...Birth: New York, N.Y., May 19, 1928...Entered NYU when only 16 and finished career as All-America...Joined the Syracuse Nationals in 1948 and for the next decade he was one of the top scorers in professional basketball and the Nats was one of the best teams...A member of the NBA all-star team 12 times as a forward, with an exciting outside touch... Scored 19,249 points and played in a one-time record 1,059 games...Later coached the Philadelphia 76ers—

formerly the Nats—and Buffalo Braves...He was coach of the year with the 76ers in 1965–66...Also served as supervisor of NBA officials.

LYNN ST. JOHN

Elected as contributor 1962...Birth: Union City, Pa., Nov. 18, 1876...Died: Sept. 30, 1950...Served on NCAA rules committee 1912–37...Chairman rules committee 1919–37...At time of first basketball competition in Olympics, prevented a split in ranks of separate factions in U.S. amateur basketball...Helped organize National Basketball Committee of U.S. and Canada...Director of Athletics, Ohio State University, 1915–47...Basketball coach, Ohio State 1912–19.

JOHN SCHOMMER

Elected as player 1959...Birth: Chicago, Ill., Jan. 29, 1884...Died: Jan. 11, 1960...All-time All-American selection by Helms Athletic Foundation...12-letterman at University of Chicago 1906–09...Four-time All-American center in basketball...His 80-foot goal gave Chicago a last-second victory for the national title over Pennsylvania in 1908...Once scored 15 field goals in game against University of Illinois...During 1908–09 season he had an amazing defensive string of nine games when he held the opposing centers to a total of four baskets.

BARNEY SEDRAN

Elected as player 1962...Birth: New York City, Jan. 28, 1891...Died: Jan. 14, 1969...Played professional basketball in Eastern United States for fifteen seasons, 1912–26...Teamed with such other immortals as Nat

Holman, John Beckman, Dutch Dehnert, Elmer Ripley, Honey Russell, Marty Friedman...Ended career with Fort Wayne and Cleveland Rosenblums...Selected on many all-time all-pro teams...Played at 118 pounds, 5-4...Coached a number of well-known teams including Brooklyn Jewels, Kate Smith Celtics, New York Whirlwinds.

AMOS ALONZO STAGG

Elected as contributor 1959...Birth: W. Orange. N.J., Aug. 16, 1862...Died: March 17, 1965...Helped James Naismith in early development of game when both were students and instructors at Springfield College... Introduced game at University of Chicago...Coached seven Western Conference basketball champions...Conducted National Interscholastic Basketball Tournament in Chicago for thirteen years...Football immortal...Hall of Famer in that sport as well.

CHRISTIAN STEINMETZ

Elected as player 1961...Birth: Milwaukee, Wis., June 28, 1882...Died: June 11, 1963..."Father" of Wisconsin basketball...One of game's earliest scoring greats at University of Wisconsin 1903–05...His following Wisconsin records were standing in 1954: most points single game (50), most field goals single game (20), most free throws single game (26), most points single season (462)...Helms Hall of Fame...Member of Wisconsin Hall of Fame.

CHARLES (CHUCK) TAYLOR

Elected as contributor 1968...Birth: Brown County, Indiana, June 24, 1901...Died: June 23, 1969...De-

veloped basketball shoe in 1921...What began as business promotion developed into career of selling basketball...Gave first basketball clinic in 1922 at North
Carolina State...Clinics took him to every major American city as well as Puerto Rico, Mexico, Hawaii,
Canada, South America, Africa and Europe...Began
Converse Rubber Co. *Yearbook* in 1922...Selected All-
American teams from 1932...Coached Air Force basketball team in World War II...Eleven-year pro career.

JOHN (CAT) THOMPSON

Elected as player 1962...Birth: St. George, Utah, Feb.
10, 1906...All-Rocky Mountain Conference selection
1927–30...1928–29 team, 36–2, led by Thompson...
Named Player of the Year by Helms Foundation...The
first real "name" player to come out of Montana area...
Also in Helms Hall of Fame.

DAVID TOBEY

Elected as referee 1961...Birth: New York City, May
1, 1898...Professional official, New York City, 1918–
25...Eastern Intercollegiate official 1926–46...Wrote
Basketball Officiating 1944...Officiated in most traditional games for many years in Madison Square Garden and Philadelphia's Convention Hall...Also a
fine professional player with the early New York
Knickerbockers and Philadelphia Spahs.

OSWALD TOWER

Elected as contributor 1959...Birth: North Adams,
Mass., Nov. 23, 1883...Died: May 28, 1968...Best
known for contributions made in interpretation of rules
...Member of rules committee 1910–59...Editor of

Basketball Guide and official rules interpreter 1915–59...Officiated for 35 years.

ARTHUR TRESTER

Elected as contributor 1961...Birth: Pecksburg, Ind., June 10, 1878...Died: Sept. 18, 1944...Commissioner of Indiana High School Athletic Association 22 years ...This Association served as model for many state organizations...Organized tournament system to play for state championship 1911.

EDWARD WACHTER

Elected as player 1961...Birth: Troy, N.Y., June 30, 1883...Died: March 12, 1966...One of the earliest professionals with Ware, Mass, team Western Professional Basketball League 1900–02...Played for many other pro teams in Massachusetts, Pennsylvania and New York including Haverhill, Mass., Pittsfield, Mass., Schenectady N.Y., McKeesport, Pa....Key man on teams that carried basketball to the hinterlands, where sport was bidding for recognition...Played center for Troy, N.Y., team that barnstormed across country to Billings, Mont....Team won 37 games on this tour...Played on more championship teams than any other player of his generation...Leading scorer Hudson River and New York State leagues for five years.

DAVID WALSH

Elected as referee 1961...Birth: Hoboken, N.J., Oct. 5, 1889...High school, college, professional official 1911–33...Associate Director, Collegiate Basketball Officials Bureau 1941–56...Secretary-treasurer International Association Approved Basketball Officials 1948–

56...Coached and taught physical education in New Jersey school system for 45 years.

W. R. CLIFFORD WELLS

Elected as contributor 1971...Birth: Indianapolis, Ind., March 17, 1896...Indiana U. graduate 1920...Began coaching career in Indiana high schools...His teams at Bloomington, Columbus and Logansport won 617 games, including 50 district, regional and invitational titles...Coached at Tulane, 1945–63...Finished with combined high-school college record of 885–418...Conducted many clinics and wrote many articles about the game...Member of national rules committee.

JOHN WOODEN

Elected as player 1960...Rehonored as coach 1972... Birth: Martinsville, Ind., Oct. 14, 1910...Three time All-American guard at Purdue 1930–32...Captained 1931–32 national-championship team...Later became one of most successful college coaches at UCLA...First coach to win five national titles and six straight from 1967 through 1972...UCLA teams won eight national titles in nine years, '64–72...Credited with developing and perfecting zone-press defense.

THE FIRST TEAM

Eighteen students from Dr. James Naismith's physical-education class participated in the first basketball game in December, 1891, at Springfield Armory YMCA, Springfield, Mass. . . . Nine players competed for each team at the same time . . . In 1897, rules stipulated that only five men could compete on one team at the same time . . . Yale defeated Pennsylvania, 32–10,

in first game played with five on side, March 20, 1897
. . . Players in the first game were: William Davis, Eu-
gene Libby, John Thompson, George Weller, Wilbert
Carey, Ernest Hildner, Lyman Archibald, T. Duncan
Patton, Finley MacDonald, Raymond Kaighn, Genza-
baro Ishikawa, Franklin Barnes, Edwin Ruggles, Frank
Mahan, William Chase, Benjamin French, George Day
and Henri Gelan.

BUFFALO GERMANS

Organized during season of 1895–96 by Frederick
Burkhardt, physical director of Buffalo German
YMCA . . . Won Pan-American Exposition in June
1901 in Buffalo on 40x60 grass court . . . Players wore
cleats . . . During season, Germans defeated Hobart
College, 134–0 . . . In 1904, won "exhibition" tournament at Olympic Games in St. Louis . . . Center Alfred
Heerdt, William Rhode, George Redlein, Alfred Man-
weiler and Edward Miller were stars of that team . . .
Though no official AAU tournaments were held between 1904 and 1910, Germans were considered best
team of period . . . Heerdt later became team manager
and guided the Germans until squad disbanded in
1929.

ORIGNAL CELTICS

Organized as the New York Celtics in 1914 by Frank
McCormack . . . Represented a settlement house on the
city's West Side . . . Pete Barry and John Witty only
members of original team that eventually played for
namesake, which gained national and international
fame . . . New York Celtics broke up before World
War I . . . Jim and Tom Furey reorganized it after
World War I, but McCormack owned rights to name

"New York Celtics," so Furey team became known as Original Celtics . . . The Celtics barnstormed the country in addition to playing in the American Pro League . . . Dutch Dehnert, Nat Holman, Chris Leonard, Johnny Beckman, Horse Haggerty, Ernie Reich, Eddie Burke, Joe Trippe, Joe Lapchick, Eddie White, Benny Borgeman and Dave Banks played for the team during its greatest days . . . Johnny Witty coached . . . From 1921 through 1929, Celtics averaged 120 victories and 10 losses . . . Won American League title twice in row, 1926–27, 1927–28, and then league broke up team, with players going to other franchises . . . Team reorganized for barnstorming purposes again in 1930s, but never attained success of earlier clubs.

NEW YORK RENS

Not until Jackie Robinson broke the color line in baseball in 1946 were black athletes accepted in organized professional sport . . . They organized their own teams, often playing the top teams of the time in exhibition games . . . The New York Rens were regarded as the best basketball team in the United States from 1932 to 1936 . . . They had an 88-game winning streak in 1933–34 . . . Organized in 1922 by Bob Douglas . . . Lasted 27 years . . . Frequently played two or three games in a day . . . Between 1932 and 1936 won 473 and lost 49 . . . Team finally broke up in 1948–49 after a 112-15 record . . . Some outstanding players included: Clarence Jenkins, Bill Yancey, John Holt, Pappy Ricks, Eyre Saitch, Charles "Tarzan" Cooper, Wee Willie Smith.